NURSERY CLASS

Other books by the same author

Win at the Tote Placepot
Tote Placepot Annual – National Hunt 2002/2003
Win at Fixed Odds Football Betting

NURSERY
CLASS

A study of two-year-old handicap races

MALCOLM BOYLE

Foreword

Tanya Stevenson

High Stakes

This edition published in June 2005 by High Stakes Publishing,
21 Great Ormond Street, London, WC1N 3JB

Distributed in the USA by Trafalgar Square Publishing, P.O. Box 257, Howe Hill
Road, North Pomfret, Vermont 05053

ISBN 1 84344 024 5

2 4 6 8 10 9 7 5 3 1

Typeset by Avocet Typeset, Chilton, Aylesbury, Bucks
Printed and bound in Great Britain by Cox & Wyman, Reading

**To Joe and Margy McNally, Simon Florence and
everyone associated with www.lazybet.com**

ACKNOWLEDGEMENTS

Sincere thanks are sent to Ion Mills and Claire Watts for the pains-taking task of formulating my dubious skills into a publication that is worthy of its place on the shelves.

Thanks also to Jonathan Turner (sportinglife.com) and Ed Comins (Tote Direct) for allowing me to entertain this work whilst still earning a living from their respective companies.

In the blame culture society where we currently reside, thanks are also sent to the tireless and low paid workers behind the scenes in racing stables up and down this green and pleasant land.

I suggest (not for the first time) that racing staff are not to blame when a horse feels like having an off day, and no, I'm not naive enough to think that every race in the ever-growing racing calendar is 100% *straight*. Thankfully, most of them are.

CONTENTS

FOREWORD

Malcolm and I first worked together when we shared the stage with Derek Thompson at the 25th toteplacepot party, on the anniversary of the birth of the nation's most popular bet at Newbury three years ago.

Malcolm became a statistician for the Channel 4 team at the Cheltenham Festival a couple of years ago, whilst continuing to write books and columns for sports magazines, culminating in his content for the Cheltenham and Aintree Festival guides this year.

I already knew of his work at sportinglife.com when we met, and as a stats and trends person myself, I quickly latched on to his methods and the good results that came from the hard work which created the service that he was providing.

The publication of *Nursery Class* adds yet more interest to the two-year-old handicap season, and it will be interesting to see how the trends and stats work out. Nursery events can be the toughest contests to call on a race card, and the information you will find in this publication cannot help but make your job easier as a punter. Any statistician will tell you that, like most pundits, you need luck in running, but arming yourself with as much information as you can secure will only enhance your prospects of beating the bookmaker.

See you soon from the other side of the television, or preferably on the racecourse!

Take care ... Tanya.

NURSERY RACES –
IN A CLASS OF THEIR OWN

An old adage in racing suggested that punters should concentrate on top weights in Nursery races, which are handicap events for two-year-olds.

Don't repeat such information to punters who followed that advice at the likes of Doncaster and Catterick last year (2004), as horses carrying the maximum burdens in their respective events finished out with the washing on several occasions at the two venues.

All eight top weights at Doncaster finished out of the frame, whilst just two horses at the top of the handicap scored for toteplacepot/each-way punters at Catterick, via twelve representatives.

We all follow a system one way or another, even if it is just our choice of newspaper or a particular website we visit from time to time.

The best system to acquire, of course, is a winning one, and like anything else in life, that scenario can only be brought about by hard work.

I have chosen to write about the subject of Nursery races, not because it is an easy option (anything but), just simply through fascination as much as anything else.

Punters have been warned down the years to avoid handicap events like the plague, yet we hear year upon year that the most popular races from the spectator's perspective are those that most easily relieve us of our hard earned money!

Two-year-old handicap races can be particularly baffling, especially those that are run late in the season, and it occurred to me that punters should have some type of ammunition with which to wage war with the bookmakers.

Most of the work that I carry out in the industry is based upon trends and statistics, and this book is no different to the other titles I have penned relating to the toteplacepot down the years.

My system is based on previous results, involving trainers, jockeys, weights and age sectors as far as the equine stars are concerned, along with starting prices and facts and stats from individual racecourses.

I make no apology for admitting that anybody could have written this book, simply because of all the time that it took to compile.

What you, as an interested punter, pay for on such occasions, is time, pure and simple. The time it takes for writers to compile the information that you want to read, in order to arm yourself with a little ammunition to take on the opposition.

We are, it is said, a mirror image of our parents. If we were mirror images of our bookmakers, we would have more chance of beating them in our daily combat against the dreaded enemy.

We need to mirror ourselves on such professionals if we are to have any chance of making our favourite sport pay, be it football, racing or golf.

By reading this book, you will at least have taken some steps to avoid pitfalls, focussing on positive trends, as opposed to the negative talk that is so easy and cheap to pick up in betting shops throughout the land.

The basic translation of the words Confucius was said to have uttered was *one see is better than a thousand hears*, which I interpret to mean that your own personal view of a race is infinitely superior to the option of listening to other *experts* talking about a contest after the event.

Digest the facts and stats in this book and argue your corner against anybody else in the two-year-old handicap market. Whether it makes you any money, of course, is entirely a different thing!

Interpretation is everything, but by learning some of the facts and stats on offer in this publication, you will equip yourself with relevant information to help tackle competitive Nursery events, which are in a class of their own.

If you need convincing, cast your mind back to the last day of the flat turf season, which fell on Saturday 6th November 2004.

Despite the help we have been offered down the years on the final day of the season (Joe Mercer winning the November Handicap at 20/1 on his last ride), we tend to steer clear of this meeting, as the jumpers swing into action, with the Paddy Power meeting at Cheltenham just a week away.

Last year however, there were more rich pickings to be made, this time in the Nursery sector.

Richard Fahey and Paul Hanagan had already teamed up to good effect throughout the campaign, and supporters were rewarded with a 16/1 winner, which paid £21.80 on the Tote.

This winner took Richard to the top of the trainers' tree in the Nursery sector, with no less than seven winners during the course of the turf season.

The result really wasn't difficult to predict.

You might also note that the last two winners of the opening Nursery race of the season followed the same course en route to winning their respective races at Pontefract.

Both horses had run unplaced in maiden races, finishing down the field in the same Listed event before winning at the West Yorkshire venue.

I would hardly class that as merely coincidental, whilst it's worth noting that the last four winners of that first race at Pontefract were all foaled between 23rd March and 16th April.

It should be noted that reference to each-way and toteplacepot betting in this book is an exact science, as only the first and second horses home in races for six runners (as an example) have been credited as placed.

This book relates *ONLY* to Nursery races that have been run on *turf*, though references are made to all weather races from time to time.

WHERE THE STATS BEGIN

Thirty-three clear market leaders and five joint or co-favourites won in the one hundred and twenty-nine Nursery races that were contested on turf in 2004.

Thirty-eight winners equates to a percentage of 29.4, which represents an exact price of 12/5 in bookmaking terms (see final chapter).

5/2 (nearest price usually relating to horse racing – 12/5 normally found in football markets) represents 28.6% of the market, which suggests that you should not have backed a favourite at less than those odds if working on last year's figures.

Backing anything shorter than 5/2 would represent poor value, though supporting a favourite at 11/4 or more would have theoretically been the correct procedure.

The figures from last year support this theory, as just eighteen winners emerged from fifty-five runners that started at 5/2 or less, which represents a percentage of 32.7, the nearest price equivalent of which, is 2/1.

Favourites starting at either 11/4 or 3/1 produced a winning ratio of 12/29 (63.1%), which equates to odds of 8/13.

The shortest priced favourite at 8/15 duly obliged, though it's worth noting that a 4/7 chance only managed to sneak into the frame.

On the positive side, from a toteplacepot perspective, just one favourite failed to make the frame from thirteen representatives when starting at odds of 5/4 or less.

The biggest priced favourite of the year was a 15/2 chance which finished in the money (3rd) at Pontefract in October, the venue that traditionally stages the first Nursery race run on turf in the season, during the opening days of July.

Three of the first five favourites won Nursery races last term, showing a healthy eight points level stake profit. Conversely, just one of the last eighteen market leaders (including 9/2 joint favourites) won in the final weeks of the season.

The performances of favourites (includes joint and co-favourites) in Nursery races on turf in 2004 are listed in the following table:

price	winners	placed	unplaced	placepot %
8/15	1	0	0	100
4/7	0	1	0	100
8/11	1	1	0	100
4/5	3	0	0	100
Evs	2	0	1	67
6/5	0	1	0	100
5/4	1	1	0	100
6/4	0	1	2	33
13/8	0	0	3	0
7/4	1	1	3	40
15/8	2	2	1	80
2/1	5	5	1	91
9/4	2	3	2	71
5/2	0	1	3	25
11/4	3	1	1	80
3/1	3	5	3	73
10/3	0	3	3	50
7/2	4	2	8	43
4/1	1	3	14	22
9/2	6	3	10	47
5/1	0	3	6	33
6/1	2	2	5	44
13/2	0	0	1	0
7/1	1	0	1	50
15/2	0	1	0	100
totals	38	40	68	53.42%

Trainers are desperate to please their owners towards the end of the year in a bid to ensure that all their boxes are full for the winter months.

The results tend to follow the pattern as horses emerge from the doldrums to produce winning form. The last three winners of Nursery races in 2004 started at 40/1—25/1—16/1!

Backing outsiders can be the quick route to the poor house however, particularly in the opening weeks of the Nursery season.

The 40/1 winner reported in the previous paragraphs was the only scorer at odds of 40/1 or more, from one hundred and fifty one representatives. Indeed, only nine horses within that price range managed to secure a toteplacepot/each-way position throughout the entire season!

To paint the picture more clearly, just four winners emerged from three hundred and forty-one runners when priced at 22/1 or more. Only twenty-two other horses managed to finish in the frame, leaving three hundred and fifteen other outsiders down the field.

From a mathematical perspective, those winners' prices of 22/1 or more (1 x 25/1—2 x 33/1—1 x 40/1) represented 84/1 chances in real terms, whilst runners representing the 22/1—150/1 price range were 12/1 shots to actually reach the frame when assessing the final figures.

Forty-six of last year's winners came into their successful Nursery races as scorers last time out.

It's also worth noting that the first fifty-eight winners in 2004 had finished no worse than fourth in their previous respective races.

Indeed, only six winners from the one hundred and twenty-nine scorers last year had finished out of the first four in their respective previous events.

The outstanding stats of the year however concerned two trainers. Sir Mark Prescott saddled just ten runners during the course of the turf Nursery season with six of them securing the gold medal, whilst David Elsworth scored with three of his five two-year-old handicap representatives.

TRAINERS UNDER THE SPOTLIGHT

Winning trainers of nursery races in 2004 along with the relevant starting prices:

Seven winners:
R. Fahey **(7/27)**: 16/1—8/1—7/1—9/2 fav—9/2—4/1—11/4 fav

27w

Six winners:
M. Bell **(6/36)**: 8/1—7/1—4/1—7/2 fav—3/1 fav—8/11 fav
N. Callaghan **(6/33)**: 15/2—9/2 fav—4/1 jt fav—7/2 jt fav— 2/1 fav—4/5 fav
M. Johnston **(6/41)**: 5/1—9/2 fav—9/2—11/4 fav—11/4 fav— 7/4 fav
J. Osborne **(6/33)**: 20/1—14/1—7/1—6/1—15/8—4/5 fav *23*
Sir M. Prescott **(6/10)**: 7/1—10/3—11/4—9/4 fav—2/1 fav— 4/5 fav

14

Five winners:
T. Easterby **(5/47)**: 33/1—9/1—13/2—4/1—3/1 *13 ₂*
R. Hannon **(5/79)**: 20/1—14/1—13/2—5/1—9/2

Three winners:
A. Berry **(3/25)**: 12/1—12/1—3/1
M. Channon **(3/63)**: 20/1—3/1 fav—11/4
D. Elsworth **(3/5)**: 14/1—12/1—6/1 co fav ✓ *3ठ*
P.D. Evans **(3/29)**: 14/1—8/1—5/1

B. Meehan (3/27): 13/2—3/1 fav—2/1 fav
B. Millman (3/24): 16/1—10/1—9/2 jt fav
K. Ryan (3/23): 5/1—5/4 fav—Evs fav
M. Tompkins (3/20): 7/1—3/1—9/4 fav

Two winners:
K. Burke (2/17): 7/1 & 6/1 fav
G. Butler (2/8): 40/1 & 3/1
P. Harris (2/9): 2/1 fav & 9/2
N. Littmoden (2/21): 33/1 & 7/2 fav
D. Loder (2/19): 12/1 & 7/2 fav
B. McMahon (2/12): 9/1 & 15/8 fav
W. Muir (2/21): 16/1 & 2/1 fav

One winner:
R. Bastiman (1/5): 11/2
R. Beckett (1/14): 14/1
J. Best (1/11): 12/1
J. Bethell (1/13): 8/1
P. Blockley (1/13): 9/2 fav
M. Brittain (1/5): 12/1
A. Carroll (1/3): 11/4 fav
P. Chapple-Hyam (1/13): 6/1
R. Charlton (1/4): Evs fav
P. D'Arcy (1/11): 8/1
J. Dunlop (1/17): 14/1
Mrs C. Dunnett (1/5): 11/2
M.W. Easterby (1/30): 25/1
J. Eustace (1/10): 10/1
R. Fisher (1/8): 7/2
J. Given (1/16): 10/1
J. Glover (1/3): 20/1
J. Gosden (1/2): 7/2
M. F. Harris (1/15): 11/1
P. Haslam (1/28): 9/1
B. Hills (1/11): 7/2

R. Hollinshead (**1/8**): 12/1
A. Jarvis (**1/7**): 10/1
M. Jarvis (**1/7**): 9/2
R. Johnson Houghton (**1/7**): 9/2 jt fav
S. Kirk (**1/24**): 8/1
W. Kittow (**1/5**): 14/1
B. Mactaggart (**1/4**): 14/1
M. Magnusson (**1/3**): 10/1
P.J. McBride (**1/3**): 25/1
P. Makin (**1/5**): 8/1
G.L. Moore (**1/11**): 20/1
G.M. Moore (**1/4**): 9/1
J.S. Moore (**1/15**): 9/2
Jedd O'Keefe (**1/4**): 16/1
J. O'Shea (**1/4**): 10/1
Mrs A. Perrett (**1/4**): 9/1
P. Phelan (**1/9**): 20/1
Sir M. Stoute (**1/6**): 7/1
Saeed Bin Suroor (**1/6**): 5/1
B. Smart (**1/18**): 12/1
V. Smith (**1/4**): 5/1
Ronald Thompson (**1/4**): 20/1
I. Wood (**1/18**): 20/1

Over leaf are the figures for the leading trainers last year, along with other handlers.

Trainer	2004	Previous 3 years	Total	Comment
Saeed bin Suroor	1–6	no runners	1–6	Keep a watchful eye for more runners from this yard
Sir M. Stoute	1–6	1–7	2–13	Retains his better 2YO for other races
M. Johnston	6–41	5–91	11–132	Improving, but not a great percentage rate
M. Channon	3–63	22–238	25–301	Poor last season by Mick's standards
B. Hills	1–11	13–90	14–101	Looking elsewhere for his winners
R. Hannon	5–79	20–253	25–332	Never ignore Richard's Nursery runners †
M. Jarvis	1–7	2–19	3–26	Michael doesn't raid these races too often
J. Gosden	1–2	5–20	6–22	Always a threat, John's record in the last three years is 6/15 †
J. Fanshawe	0–1	0–7	0–8	Discarded until showing signs of interest
J. Dunlop	1–17	9–53	10–70	Poor record last year by John's standards
L. Cumani	no runners	3–16	3–16	Not a great record by any means, but keep an eye open for any runners
T. Easterby	5–47	14–195	19–242	Too many runners performing badly to warrant investment
D. Nicholls	0–4	0–6	0–10	Surprisingly little interest shown by Dandy
B. Meehan	3–27	12–120	15–147	Brian's three winners occurred over just two days in the entire season!
E. Dunlop	0–18	3–44	3–62	Appalling effort last year after previous disappointing figures
D. Elsworth	3–5	0–12	3–17	David has seen the light!
A. O'Brien	no runners	no runners	no runners	If the Irish maestro saddles a runner – back it!
Mrs A. Perrett	1–4	1–9	2–13	Progressive figures

Trainer	2004	Previous 3 years	Total	Comment
R. Fahey	7–27	1–43	8–70	Fantastic effort from 'head boy' Fahey!
C. Brittain	0–10	3–22	3–32	Poor effort last year after being worth following in previous seasons
A. Balding	0–11	1–10	1–21	No interest from Andrew as far as decent representatives are concerned
P. Cole	0–8	11–46	11–54	Surprisingly poor returns last year, don't give up on the trainer just yet though
K. Ryan	3–23	5–63	8–86	Not bad figures from an underrated handler
M. Bell	6–36	7–49	13–85	Michael always takes these races seriously
M. Tregoning	no runners	2–11	2–11	Keep a watchful eye for Tregoning raiders
W. Haggas	0–1	1–28	1–29	Poor record from this yard down the years
R. Charlton	1–4	4–14	5–18	Roger's record last year was disappointing after useful previous stats
N. Littmoden	2–21	10–82	12–103	Nick seems to have lost his way on turf with his 2YO handicappers
J. Bradley	0–8	0–9	0–17	Milton doesn't seem to take these races seriously
P. Harris	2–9	1–17	3–26	It will be worth watching Walter Swinburn's raiders this term
Sir M. Prescott	6–10	12–40	18–50	Let the figures do the talking! Phenomenal effort last term after a slightly disappointing previous year
H. Morrison	0–3	3–13	3–16	Disappointing that Hughie didn't saddle more runners last term
J. Noseda	0–2	2–10	2–12	Both of Jeremy's winners came in 2003

Trainer	2004	Previous 3 years	Total	Comment
M. Tompkins	3–20	4–35	7–55	Back to winning ways for Mark and his team following two year figures of 0–19
T. David Barron	0–25	7–64	7–89	A wretched year for David Barron's Nursery contenders
G. Butler	2–8	1–16	3–24	Much better figures from Gerard Butler last term—worth keeping on the right side
H. Candy	0–2	1–4	1–6	Barely worth watching at present
D. Loder	2–19	1–7	3–26	David produces fair figures from his lesser lights
G. Wragg	0–1	1–2	1–3	Geoff's lone winner was a 25/1 chance, so don't write off the old scoundrel just yet!
S. Kirk	1–24	4–40	5–64	Quick route to the poor house
P. D. Evans	3–29	5–55	8–84	You can rarely ignore David's two-year-old contenders
P. Chapple-Hyam	1–13	no runners	1–13	Not a bad first year back for this popular handler
K. Burke	2–17	0–44	2–61	Karl finally started to get to grips with his two-year-old handicappers
W. Muir	2–21	0–26	2–47	Definite improvement last term, though that would not have been difficult to achieve!
G. L. Moore	1–11	0–8	1–19	A 20/1 winner emerged last year, and don't be surprised if Gary sends out more Nursery raiders this term
N. Callaghan	6–33	16–84	22–117	It's always worth keeping Neville's runners on the right side, particularly at Newmarket

Trainer	2004	Previous 3 years	Total	Comment
B. McMahon	2–12	6–35	8–47	Bryan continued to excel with his two-year-olds from his small yard – licence now held by son Ed.
J. J. Quinn	0–20	1–30	1–50	It doesn't take a mathematician to work out that a 50/1 winner would merely produce a minor profit!
A. Berry	3–25	5–145	8–170	The two previous years had returned figures of 0–88; hence Alan's controversial season was not all doom and gloom
J. Osborne	6–33	14–57	20–90	If only all trainers would follow Jamie's example! Figures over the last two years read 18/70
J. Given	1–12	2–36	3–52	Disappointing figures from James and his team
W. Brisbourne	0–10	1–8	1–18	Hardly worth keeping on the right side
B. Smart	1–18	5–43	6–61	A poor year followed just average figures during the study period
M. W. Easterby	1–30	3–63	4–93	The figures just don't stack up these days for Mick and his team
C. Wall	0–3	0–3	0–6	Nothing worth noting
John Oxx	no runners	no runners	no runners	Not likely to be any runners in this sector from this stable
P. Makin	1–5	1–4	2–9	Worth keeping on the right side
J. Bethell	1–13	2–26	3–39	Just average figures to report I'm afraid
P. Blockley	1–13	0–9	1–22	Paul continues to centre his efforts towards sand
E. J. Alston	0–4	0–13	0–17	Somewhat surprising that Eric does not do better with his Nursery raiders

Trainer	2004	Previous 3 years	Total	Comment
I. Semple	0–3	0–13	0–16	Things have got to improve
Miss Gay Kelleway	no runners	0–2	0–2	Continues to raid the all-weather tracks to good effect
J. Best	1–11	3–45	4–56	The Maidstone branch disappointed in this sector of the game last term
S. C. Williams	no runners	no runners	no runners	Watch for a runner from this shrewd stable
D. Chapman	0–3	0–4	0–7	Disappointing number of entries and results from this stable
H. Cecil	no runners	0–2	0–2	Words fail me when talking of Henry's recent fortunes
R. Hollinshead	1–8	0–23	1–31	Reg is one of the gamest trainers in the business—unlike a lot of his horses!
B. Ellison	0–6	0–5	0–11	Brian doesn't raid these races too often and results are disappointing
A. Carroll	1–3	1–6	2–9	Tony does reasonably well with his rare raiders in this sector of the sport
B. Millman	3–24	1–46	4–70	Things had to improve, and they did @ 16/1—10/1—9/2!
J. Hills	0–4	0–21	0–25	There are not too many worse records than this to report—thankfully!
J. Goldie	0–2	0–23	0–25	Jim doesn't seem interested in these races
J. Howard Johnson	0–4	no runners	0–4	I guess there will be more runners in this sector this term—keep a watchful eye
Mrs J. Ramsden	0–19	3–40	3–59	The last two seasons show figures of 0–32 which is unacceptable for a stable of this size

Trainer	2004	Previous 3 years	Total	Comment
J. Akehurst	no runners	0–5	0–5	Little to report
D. Ivory	0–1	1–9	1–10	Dean doesn't show much interest in these events
M. Dods	0–12	2–11	2–23	A disappointing year after fair figures in the previous two terms
G. Balding	0–2	0–25	0–27	Toby will be missed, but not from this sector of racing!
R. Guest	0–4	0–9	0–13	No positive news to report
T. Mills	0–5	0–3	0–8	I'm surprised that Terry doesn't have more Nursery runners
D. Flood	no runners	1–6	1–6	Keep an eye out for any Nursery raiders this term
W. Jarvis	0–5	0–20	0–25	Willie just doesn't cut the rug in this sector of the game
G. A. Swinbank	0–3	3–9	3–12	Let's hope for a return to previous efforts this term. Stable worth watching
J. Eustace	1–10	3–11	4–21	Although the figures show a decline, James places his horses to good effect in the main
P. Haslam	1–28	6–43	7–71	A poor year last term from a trainer with previous good figures
P. Chamings	0–2	0–4	0–6	Little to report
B. Powell	0–1	0–4	0–5	I'm expecting more runners from the yard this term after a good winter
I. Wood	1–18	4–38	5–56	A 20/1 winner bailed the stable out of trouble last term!
P. Hiatt	no runners	no runners	no runners	Watch out for any representatives
J. Jenkins	0–2	1–4	1–6	Disappointing that only two runners emerged from the stable last year

Trainer	2004	Previous 3 years	Total	Comment
A. Jarvis	1–7	2–39	3–46	A 10/1 winner helped to produce black figures last term
M. Quinlan	0–8	2–14	2–22	Connections would have been disappointed by last years figures in this sector
Andrew Reid	0–3	0–9	0–12	Andrew's runners continue to disappoint in two-year-old handicap events
Jamie Poulton	no runners	0–2	0–2	Little to report
G. G. Margarson	0–6	3–32	3–38	I wouldn't totally write GG off just yet
Stef Liddiard	no runners	0–2	0–2	Little to report
M. Magnusson	1–3	1–1	2–4	A yard to watch out for in Nursery events, a 10/1 winner emerged last term †
R. Beckett	1–14	8–58	9–72	A poor year by Ralph's standards
R. Bastiman	1–5	0–4	1–9	Making slow progress
M. Brittain	1–5	2–5	3–10	Worth keeping an eye on Brittain's few Nursery contenders ←
P. D'Arcy	1–11	0–7	1–18	Hardly scintillating stats last year—though an improvement on previous figures
Mrs C. Dunnett	1–5	0–6	1–11	A 20% record is always classed as successful in this sport
R. Fisher	1–8	0–6	1–14	Little to note with a level one pound stake loss of £3.50
J. Glover	1–3	0–18	1–21	A 20/1 winner kept the books balanced last year
M. F. Harris	1–15	0–4	1–19	It took a decent number of runners to produce the one (11/1) winner

Trainer	2004	Previous 3 years	Total	Comment
R. Johnson Houghton	1–7	4–40	5–47	A winning 9/2 joint favourite couldn't prevent red figures
W. Kittow	1–5	0–3	1–8	A 14/1 winner at Chepstow kept the dream alive last year
J. S. Moore	1–15	4–34	5–49	Winners are the name of the game, though the percentage figures are ordinary
P. J. McBride	1–3	0–1	1–4	A 25/1 winner kept the landlord at bay!
B. Mactaggart	1–4	no runners	1–4	Worth keeping an eye on this small yard that sent out a 10/1 winner last term
G. M. Moore	1–4	1–24	2–28	George improved his ratio considerably last season
Jedd O'Keefe	1–4	0–7	1–11	A 16/1 winner kept the wolves at bay
J. O'Shea	1–4	1–6	2–10	Last two seasons show 2/7 figures which make for good reading
P. Phelan	1–9	no runners	1–9	A 20/1 winner helped to record a healthy level stake profit
V. Smith	1–4	no runners	1–4	A yard we are going to hear a lot more about in the years to come
Ronald Thompson	1–4	0–5	1–9	Going the right way

Here are the full 2004 Nursery stats for six leading trainers.

Richard Fahey:

Racecourse	winners	placed runners	unplaced runners	placepot %
Ayr	0	0	7/2	Nil
Carlisle	0	0	6/1	Nil
Catterick	0	11/4	50/1—8/1	33
Chester	8/1—11/4f	9/4	9/2	75
Doncaster	16/1	0	0	100
Haydock	9/2f	0	0	100
Musselburgh	0	0	6/1	Nil
Newmarket (RM)	0	0	14/1	Nil
Newmarket (July)	0	7/1	8/1	50
Pontefract	0	0	7/1	Nil
Redcar	9/2	0	5/1f—16/1	33
Ripon	4/1	0	13/2	50
Sandown	0	0	11/4	Nil
Thirsk	7/1	0	0	100
Warwick	0	0	14/1	Nil
York	0	0	4/1—7/1—12/1	Nil

Neville Callaghan:

Racecourse	winners	placed runners	unplaced runners	placepot %
Ascot	0	15/8f	14/1	50
Catterick	0	4/1f	16/1—5/1	33
Doncaster	0	0	9/1—33/1	Nil
Epsom	0	0	16/1	Nil
Goodwood	0	0	9/2	Nil
Leicester	0	0	14/1	Nil
Lingfield	4/5f	10/1	0	100
Newmarket (RM)	15/2	7/1	40/1	33
Newmarket (July)	7/2jf	10/1	16/1—40/1—16/1	40

Racecourse	winners	placed runners	unplaced runners	placepot %
Nottingham	9/2f	0	0	100
Pontefract	0	18/1	0	100
Redcar	0	0	20/1	Nil
Sandown	0	0	12/1	Nil
Warwick	4/1jf	0	0	100
Windsor	0	0	6/4f—4/1f	Nil
Yarmouth	2/1f	0	66/1—7/1f	33
York	0	0	16/1	Nil

Mark Johnston:

Racecourse	winners	placed runners	unplaced runners	placepot %	
Ascot	0	10/3	0	100	
Ayr	9/2	4/1	10/3f—12/1	50	—
Beverley	11/4f	0	0	100	—
Catterick	7/4f—9/2f	0	7/2f—5/2f—5/1	40	—
Doncaster	5/1	10/1	10/1—10/1	50	—
Epsom	0	0	16/1	Nil	
Goodwood	0	15/2	6/1	50	
Hamilton	0	5/2f	7/1	50	
Haydock	0	0	25/1	Nil	
Musselburgh	8/15f	7/2	9/1	67	
Newbury	0	6/1	20/1	50	
Newmarket (RM)	0	0	7/1—14/1—10/1—33/1	Nil	
Newmarket (July)	0	4/1f	5/1	50	
Pontefract	0	5/4f	10/1	50	
Redcar	0	0	33/1	Nil	
Ripon	0	0	3/1f	Nil	
Salisbury	0	0	13/8f	Nil	
Windsor	0	14/1	0	100	
Yarmouth	0	0	14/1	Nil	
York	0	0	20/1—9/2f	Nil	

Jamie Osborne:

Racecourse	winners	placed runners	unplaced runners	placepot %
Ascot	0	0	9/2—16/1	Nil
Bath	0	0	12/1	Nil
Brighton	4/5f	0	0	100
Catterick	0	0	11/1	Nil
Chepstow	15/8f	0	0	100
Doncaster	20/1	0	4/1f—7/4f	33
Epsom	0	0	9/1	Nil
Goodwood	0	7/4f	9/1	50
Kempton	0	0	10/1	Nil
Lingfield	7/1—6/1	0	11/1—10/1	50
Musselburgh	0	5/1jf	0	100
Newbury	0	0	7/1—10/1—16/1 —8/1	Nil
Newmarket (July)	0	0	14/1	Nil
Nottingham	0	66/1	0	100
Ripon	0	0	9/1	Nil
Thirsk	0	0	4/1	Nil
Warwick	0	9/2—2/1f	7/4f	67
Windsor	14/1	0	0	100
Yarmouth	0	0	33/1—16/1	Nil
York	0	11/1	0	100

Mick Channon:

Racecourse	winners	placed runners	unplaced runners	placepot %
Ayr	0	3/1f	16/1	50
Bath	0	0	7/1	Nil
Brighton	0	6/1	12/1	50
Catterick	0	0	12/1—11/1— 16/1—16/1—22/1	Nil
Chepstow	0	0	7/2—7/1	Nil
Chester	0	0	12/1—9/4f	Nil
Doncaster	11/4F	20/1—12/1	40/1—14/1	60
Epsom	3/1F	0	0	100

Racecourse	winners	placed runners	unplaced runners	placepot %
Goodwood	0	10/3f	20/1—7/4f—4/1—66/1—25/1—33/1	14
Haydock	0	7/2—10/1	0	100
Kempton	0	0	16/1	Nil
Lingfield	0	0	33/1—50/1	Nil
Newbury	0	0	12/1—33/1	Nil
Newcastle	0	9/1	16/1—7/2jf	33
Newmarket (RM)	20/1	0	16/1—20/1—25/1—6/1f	20
Newmarket (July)	0	50/1—14/1—7/2jf	7/1	75
Nottingham	0	0	14/1	Nil
Pontefract	0	7/2	0	100
Redcar	0	0	4/1f—5/1f	Nil
Salisbury	0	25/1	6/1co fav of 4	50
Sandown	0	9/2	0	100
Windsor	0	0	25/1—14/1	Nil
Yarmouth	0	11/2—40/1	33/1—40/1—14/1	40
York	0	0	11/2—15/2	Nil

Richard Hannon:

Racecourse	winners	placed runners	unplaced runners	placepot %
Ascot	0	11/2	13/2—12/1	33
Bath	0	10/3f	9/1—10/1	33
Brighton	0	0	10/1	Nil
Chepstow	0	8/11f—3/1	4/1—4/1	50
Chester	0	0	9/2	Nil
Doncaster	0	11/1	9/2jf—7/1—20/1—25/1—50/1	17
Epsom	0	0	4/1f	Nil
Folkestone	0	0	7/2	Nil
Goodwood	13/2—5/1	14/1	33/1—33/1—25/1—25/1—16/1	38
Haydock	20/1	0	0	100

Racecourse	winners	placed runners	unplaced runners	placepot %
Kempton	14/1	0	0	100
Leicester	0	0	33/1—14/1	Nil
Lingfield	0	0	6/1jf—8/1—33/1 —20/1	Nil
Newbury	0	0	18/1—10/1— 14/1—25/1	Nil
Newmarket (RM)	0	16–5–16– 10–20	6/1—12/1	71
Newmarket (July)	0	11/2— 8/1—5/2	33–14–20–14– 13/2–8–16–10–7	25
Nottingham	0	5/1—11/1	0	100
Pontefract	0	16/1	10/1	50
Salisbury	0	10/1	6/1cf of 4	50
Sandown	0	0	25/1	Nil
Warwick	0	8/1	0	100
Windsor	9/2	0	4/1f—16/1	33 -
Yarmouth	0	0	50/1	Nil
York	0	13/2	11/1	50

AT-A-GLANCE TABLES

The weights that horses carried throughout the Nursery year produced the following results:

weight	races won	placed	unplaced	placepot%
9–13	0	1	0	100
9–12	0	0	1	0
9–11	2	0	1	67
9–10	0	1	0	100
9–9	0	0	2	0
9–8	2	0	1	67
9–7	11	24	86	29
9–6	7	11	33	35
9–5	4	7	31	26
9–4	7	12	34	36
9–3	8	16	36	40
9–2	6	14	62	24
9–1	5	11	36	31
9–0	11	14	54	32
8–13	7	21	54	34
8–12	8	15	68	25
8–11	4	18	65	25
8–10	1	11	61	16
8–9	1	13	59	19
8–8	10	13	40	36
8–7	3	7	53	16
8–6	6	11	71	19
8–5	3	11	47	23

weight	races won	placed	unplaced	placepot%
8–4	5	4	49	15
8–3	8	7	24	38
8–2	2	4	27	18
8–1	2	6	34	19
8–0	0	4	32	11
7–13	3	3	30	17
7–12	3	6	42	18
7–11	0	2	9	18
7–10	0	0	6	0
7–9	0	2	15	11
7–8	0	0	1	0
7–7	0	1	8	11
7–6	0	2	6	25
7–5	0	0	8	0

STARTING PRICE DETAILS:

As an example, forty-two horses started at 9/1. Five of them won, twelve were placed and twenty-five finished out of the frame, creating a toteplacepot percentage of 40 (rounded down).

price	races won	placed	unplaced	placepot%
8–15	1	0	0	100
4–7	0	1	0	100
8–11	1	1	0	100
4–5	3	0	0	100
Evs	2	0	1	66
6–5	0	1	0	100
5–4	1	1	0	100
6–4	0	1	2	33
13–8	0	0	3	0
7–4	1	1	3	40
15–8	2	2	1	80
2–1	5	5	1	91
9–4	2	4	3	66
5–2	0	3	3	50
11–4	5	2	2	78

weight	races won	placed	unplaced	placepot%
3–1	7	7	6	70
10–3	1	4	5	50
7–2	7	6	16	45
4–1	4	10	37	27
9–2	12	12	23	51
5–1	6	10	22	42
11–2	2	6	8	50
6–1	4	12	29	35
13–2	3	6	20	31
7–1	7	14	52	29
15–2	1	5	10	37
8–1	7	15	41	35
17–2	0	0	3	0
9–1	5	12	25	40
10–1	7	22	79	27
11–1	1	12	28	32
12–1	8	12	83	19
14–1	7	14	102	17
16–1	4	29	107	23
18–1	0	1	2	33
20–1	8	12	110	15
22–1	0	1	5	16
25–1	2	13	104	13
28–1	0	0	12	0
33–1	2	5	100	6
40–1	1	5	33	15
50–1	0	3	63	4
66–1	0	1	34	3
80–1	0	0	2	0
100–1	0	0	7	0
150–1	0	0	2	0

TOP WEIGHTS:

Over leaf was the record of top weighted horses in races at the respective meetings. Two of the three top weighted horses at Epsom finished in the frame for example, including one winner at 3/1.

Racecourse	Placepot record	winners
Newmarket (July)	4–8	7/2 jf
Ayr	3–6	9/2 & 10/3
Chepstow	3–6	11/4f—15/8 f & 2/1f
Goodwood	3–6	
Brighton	2–2	4/5f
Bath	2–3	
Epsom	2–3	3/1f
Pontefract	2–4	7/2
Redcar	2–4	
Chester	2–5	8/1
Nottingham	2–5	2/1f
Musselburgh	2–5	8/15f
Haydock	2–6	
York	2–7	7/2
Catterick	2–12	9/2f
Carlisle	1–1	
Folkestone	1–1	
Ascot	1–2	
Kempton	1–2	
Newbury	1–3	
Hamilton	1–4	
Leicester	1–4	Evsf
Newcastle	1–4	
Windsor	1–5	
Newmarket (RM)	1–6	
Yarmouth	1–7	
Thirsk	0–1	
Beverley	0–2	
Ripon	0–2	
Sandown	0–2	
Salisbury	0–3	
Warwick	0–3	
Lingfield	0–6	
Doncaster	0–8	

FAVOURITES (including joint and co-favourites):
As an example, three of the six favourites were placed at Yarmouth, including two winners at 9/4 and 2/1.

Racecourse	Placepot record	winners
Newmarket (July)	6–9	7/2jf—7/2f—9/4f & 8/11f
Bath	4–4	9/2jf
Chepstow	4–4	2/1f—15/8f & 11/8f
Goodwood	4–6	
Lingfield	4–6	7/1f & 4/5f
Newmarket (RM)	4–6	3/1—2/1 & 15/8
Catterick	4–7	9/2 & 7/4
Nottingham	3–4	9/2f—2/1f & 5/4f
Chester	3–5	7/2f—11/4f & Evsf
Ayr	3–6	
Yarmouth	3–6	9/4f & 2/1f
Musselburgh	3–6	4/5f & 8/15f
Haydock	3–6	9/2f
Leicester	3–6	9/2jf & Evsf
Doncaster	3–9	
Ascot	2–2	3/1f
Brighton	2–2	4/5f
Hamilton	2–3	9/2f
Newcastle	2–4	6/1f
Pontefract	2–4	
Warwick	2–4	4/1jf
Carlisle	1–1	
Folkestone	1–1	
Thirsk	1–1	
Beverley	1–2	11/4f
Epsom	1–2	3/1f
Sandown	1–2	2/1f
Kempton	1–3	
Newbury	1–3	
Redcar	1–4	
Salisbury	1–5	6/1 co fav of 4
Windsor	1–5	
York	1–6	7/2f
Ripon	0–2	

THE 129 NURSERY WINNERS ON TURF IN 2004

The following results are listed to give you an indication of where the winners were sent after victory, on the back of what the horses had previously achieved. You might care to remember these names for 2005.

6th July PONTEFRACT
Won by **Prospect Court** (Pivotal—Scierpan)
Foaled on 11th April
Trained by J. Bethell—ridden by T. Quinn

The Nursery season started at Pontefract as usual, with the winner having been dropped down in grade after contesting a Listed event at Ascot on his previous outing. Prospect Court had also claimed a toteplacepot position via two other efforts prior to this victory, and this was his first step up in trip after tackling three races over the minimum distance. James Bethell's winner went on to contest four further races during the course of the season without troubling the judge, albeit that Prospect Court was raised in class after lifting this prize.

7th July LINGFIELD
Won by **Lateral Thinker** (Desert Fun—Miss Margate)
Foaled on 20th April
Trained by J. Osborne—ridden by S. Kelly

Lateral Thinker had been placed in his two efforts on turf before this race, but only went on to lift a seller at Wolverhampton later in the year. Five efforts on turf followed this victory without any reward for each-way punters; joined David Evans after winning the seller.

8th July NEWMARKET (JULY)
Won by **Satchem** (Inchinor—Mohican Princess)
Foaled on 11th February
Trained by D. Loder—ridden by T. Queally

Satchem's win was the middle leg of a well-earned hat trick, which had been initiated with a maiden victory at Yarmouth on firm ground. The victory here was gained on good-to-soft so the winner is nothing if not genuine. Has joined Godolphin.

9th July CHESTER
Won by **Nova Tor** (Trans Island—Nordic Living)
Foaled on 24th April
Trained by N. Littmoden—ridden by I. Mongan

Another David Evans' raider (from stall 8) thwarted a clean sweep for the inside runners in a typical sprint race at Chester which is so often dictated by the draw. Nova Tor had started his career by winning at Southwell on his debut, and went on to win three races on turf (including another Nursery) from twelve appearances. Nick Littmoden's raider was considered good enough to tackle quality races at The Curragh and Newmarket (without success) on his last two turf starts of the season.

10th July ASCOT
Won by **Sacred Nuts** (Sri Pekan—Sagrada)
Foaled on 3rd March
Trained by M. Bell—ridden by L. Dettori

Sacred Nuts had previously scored at Hamilton after showing promise at Doncaster first time out in June. Although only beaten by an aggregate of less than seven lengths in three subsequent outings, Sacred Nuts only secured one place position in the process. Two Richard Hannon raiders contested this event which turned out to be disappointing types later in the season, having been well thought of at home.

10th July YORK
Won by **Key Secret** (Whittingham—Foxkey)
Foaled on 7th March
Trained by M. Bell—ridden by A. McCarthy

Michael Bell was fast out of the traps in the Nursery sector as usual, and despite an official going report of good, Key Secret enjoyed this easier ground, which was confirmed later in the season when scoring at Windsor in genuine good-to-soft conditions. This was the third win from as many starts for Key Secret, though just the one Windsor victory emerged from six subsequent efforts on turf. The Whittingham filly had a one hundred per cent record on sand at the time of writing.

15th July LEICESTER
Won by **Colonel Bilko** (General Monash—Mari-Ela)
Foaled on 11th February
Trained by B. Millman—ridden by F. Norton

Colonel Bilko was placed on his first effort at Folkestone in March, but this victory was the only other cheque he won for connections via just five races during the season. Beating a subsequent Nursery winner (Safendonseabiscuit) at Leicester, Colonel Bilko finished last of ten on his only further visit to a racecourse.

16th July HAMILTON
Won by **No Commission** (General Monash—Price Of Passion)
Foaled on 7th February
Trained by R. Fisher—ridden by R. Winston

It was generally considered that the two experienced jockeys in the line up (Robert Winston and Joe Fanning) determined the outcome of this event, as they ignored the breakneck pace the other runners were creating. No Commission was franking the form of Shamardal, who had beaten this winner by a facile eight lengths at Ayr, the only occasion that Roger Fisher's raider was able to claim a toteplacepot position from eleven other races during the campaign.

17th July HAYDOCK
Won by **Make Us Flush** (Mind Games—Pearls)
Foaled on 14th February
Trained by A. Berry—ridden by F. Norton

Having shown little in her first four races, Make Us Flush was surprisingly returned as the market leader in her previous race, though softer ground proved to be the key to the filly. Make Us Flush went on to win a subsequent Nursery at Haydock on heavy-going in August, having scored on soft ground here. Apart from her three victories, Alan Berry's juvenile only claimed one other toteplacepot position from nine other races.

17th July LINGFIELD
Won by **Forzeen** (Forzando—Mazurkanova)
Foaled on 5th March
Trained by J. Osborne—ridden by E. Ahern

Forzeen enjoyed a better record on the all-weather courses, but also went on to win another Nursery event at Windsor in September. Forzeen had only been narrowly beaten by the useful juvenile yardstick The Crooked Ring in his previous run on turf, and 6/1 was a slightly generous return in my book. The subsequent victory at Windsor was the only bright spot in the book following this win however, as four poor efforts were recorded before and after scoring at the royal venue.

19th July BRIGHTON
Won by **Whatatodo** (Compton Place—Emerald Dream)
Foaled on 6th April
Trained by M. Bell—ridden by J. Quinn

Having been placed in one of her first three efforts, the winner went on to contest a better race at Newmarket when finishing second, though that effort was easily the best of her remaining races. Whatatodo was beating four winners here however, though winning off an official mark of 62 probably best sums up the filly. That having been said, any jeuvenile that can handle the undulations at Brighton on fast ground is alright by me.

19th July AYR
Won by **The Crooked Ring** (Magic Ring—My Bonus)
Foaled on 13th March
Trained by P.D. Evans—ridden by R. Winston

The form was in the book for all to see (look at the comment for Forzeen on July 17), yet a price of 8/1 was returned for this useful Magic Ring gelding. The Crooked Ring had already won at Warwick, whilst recording two other placed efforts via seven starts prior to this event. The David Evans' raider went on to claim another Nursery race after this victory before taking on Listed company later in the season. Having run creditably from April right through to October, The Crooked Ring was one of the most consistent juvenile performers during the course of the season.

21st July CATTERICK
Won by **Jane Jubilee** (Mister Baileys—Elsie Bamford)
Foaled on 19th February
Trained by M. Johnston—ridden by J. Fanning

A typical Mister Baileys type (tough and genuine), Jane Jubilee ran out a decent five lengths winner, with future Nursery scorer Paris Bell well down the field. Having finished as runner-up in her two previous races, Jane Jubilee went on to win her next (Nursery) event before tackling some tough races where she was far from disgraced. Her dam ran unplaced as a juvenile but became a very useful type going on to take several staying events. Jane Jubilee could be one to note as a three-year-old.

21st July LEICESTER
Won by **Brag** (Mujadil—Boast)
Foaled on 26th March
Trained by R. Charlton—ridden by D. Sweeney

Brag was arguably harshly treated by the handicapper for winning this event, as Roger Charlton's juvenile was raised from a mark of 72 to 82 for a mere one length victory. Brag finished third in her next outing before running down the field in another grade 'C' event. The Mujadil filly had started the season by running second in a reasonable event at Salisbury, but her season only lasted until August, taking in just six races in the process.

22nd July DONCASTER
Won by **Bibury Flyer** (Zafonic—Affair Of State)
Foaled on 12th February
Trained by M. Channon—ridden by S. Hitchcott

The winner was totally exposed as a juvenile, and I cannot pretend that I approve of a two-year-old running twenty times between March and October. I readily admit that all horses are different, and some take their racing better than others, but I would be surprised if Bibury Flyer went on to achieve a great deal as a three-year-old, irrespective of the fact that the Zafonic filly ran well 'out East' when beaten less than ten lengths by Satin Kiss in February. What I cannot deny, however, is that Mick Channon's raider claimed three victories and six placed efforts during the course of her first season. She must be tough. Now with Jeremy Noseda.

23rd July NEWMARKET(JULY)
Won by **Silver Wraith** (Danehill Dancer—Alpine Lady)
Foaled on 19th March
Trained by N. Callaghan—ridden by J. Murtagh

A thoroughly admirable (typically Danehill Dancer) type, Silver Wraith was winning his third race of the season when claiming this Nursery event off top weight. Placed in three of his other five races, Neville Callaghan's raider got the seven furlongs really well and might get as far as a mile in time. The trainer called it quits after a thirteen week season, and there could be plenty more to come from Michael Tabor's representative.

24th July YORK
Won by **Mimi Mouse** (Diktat—Shifty Mouse)
Foaled on 17th March
Trained by T. Easterby—ridden by K. Darley

Mimi Mouse was hiked in class after two victories, and the Diktat filly followed up a modest Pontefract success in good style here. Previously beaten just half a length at York, Mimi Mouse was showing much improved form after two modest efforts earlier in the season. Both her victories were gained on good-to-firm ground over the minimum trip, whilst her two efforts at six furlongs produced little to encourage connections to try again.

28th July KEMPTON
Won by **The Crooked Ring** (Magic Ring—My Bonus)
Foaled on 13th March
Trained by P.D. Evans—ridden by S. Donohoe

Another good performance by the winner (see comment for 19th July), The Crooked Ring ran on the favoured side of the course as the first five home ran down the stands side of the track. This does not detract from another impressive performance however, and whilst the Magic Ring gelding is far from top class, he is nonetheless a thoroughly likeable sort who could become a good journeyman for connections.

29th July MUSSELBURGH
Won by **Jane Jubilee** (Mister Baileys—Elsie Bamford)
Foaled on 19th February
Trained by M. Johnston—ridden by S. Chin

The Nursery form was beginning to stand up now, and Jane Jubilee (see comment for 21st July) confirmed the promise that had been shown throughout the opening months of the season. Winning by two lengths and six, Stanley Chin's mount offset the burden of 9–11 in heroic style. Eight to ten furlongs will be her trip in all probability.

31st July GOODWOOD
Won by **Easy Feeling** (Night Shift—Talena)
Foaled on 25th February
Trained by R. Hannon—ridden by R.L. Moore

Having finished third on her first effort at Haydock over six furlongs, Easy Feeling ran a couple of disappointing races before stepping back up to this trip. She ran unplaced in her two closing outings in the season, but was not beaten far (seven lengths) behind the useful Swan Nebula over seven furlongs at Doncaster in a decent race in September. Another positive point to note is that Richard Hannon's raider was beating Bibury Flyer here by the thick end of three lengths, which was no bad performance from a similar mark to Mick Channon's exposed representative.

31st July GOODWOOD
Won by **Keep Bacckinhit** (Raise A Grand—Taispeain)
Foaled on 30th March
Trained by G.L. Moore—ridden by Lisa Jones

The winner was a 20/1 chance on the back of some ordinary performances before this event, albeit that Gary Moore's raider had finished third in a moderate contest at Windsor immediately prior to this success. Unplaced in four subsequent races, Keep Bacckinhit might have benefited from a rough race, which could have produced any amount of different results in the circumstances.

31st July HAMILTON
Won by **Borderlescott** (Compton Place—Jeewan)
Foaled on 21st April
Trained by R. Bastiman—ridden by P. Hanagan

Having been placed in just one of his three previous starts, Borderlescott seemed to appreciate the extra (sixth) furlong, and Paul Hanagan's mount ran out a decent winner from a (six strong) field that was stretched out by the time the winner crossed the finish line. Although the favourite (Propellor) was a little short of room a few furlongs from home, Alan Dickman's raider would never have beaten the winner, and the Compton Place colt was 'retired' for the season after this victory.

31st July NEWMARKET(JULY)
Won by **Transaction** (Trans Island—Meranie Girl)
Foaled on 13th March
Trained by J. Eustace—ridden by S. Drowne

Transaction was following up a decent York maiden success
when taking this event, and although the first eight horses
home finished in something of a heap, Steve Drowne's mount
showed battling qualities. Both his victories (and his runner-up
position at Leicester) were gained over six furlongs, and this is
very much a sprinter in the making, who is a half brother to the
useful Cheverak Forest.

31st July THIRSK
Won by **Wise Wager** (Titus Livius—Londubh)
Foaled on 17th March
Trained by R. Fahey—ridden by P. Hanagan

Having been placed in her four previous races (including one
on sand), Wise Wager was hardly winning out of turn, and
overcoming a poor draw, she stayed on really well to score for
Richard Fahey and Paul Hanagan, who were to go on and claim
many more Nursery events throughout the season. Wise
Wager went on to run well again on her next two outings
before running down the field at Musselburgh on her last
appearance. It's never easy to predict what will happen after a
two-year-old has enjoyed a good opening term, especially when
discussing fillies.

1st Aug CHESTER
Won by **Golden Legacy** (Rossini—Dissidentia)
Foaled on 4th April
Trained by R. Fahey—ridden by P. Hanagan

Golden Legacy had finished second on firm ground at the first
time of asking at Redcar in June, and was following up a decent

maiden victory on similar good-to-firm going at Catterick. The winner went on to score again on soft ground later on in the season, and the Rossini filly is a thoroughly reliable type.

1st Aug NEWBURY
Won by **King Of Blues** (Bluebird—Highly Respected)
Foaled on 10th February
Trained by M. Magnusson—ridden by E. Ahern

Unplaced in four of his six starts, King Of Blues is reportedly a lazy (though not ungenuine) type, though this might not have been one of the strongest Nursery races ever run at Newbury. It could be argued that King Of Blues did well to win over seven furlongs, as his future looks to be over races in excess of eight furlongs. Third in his last race at 'headquarters', Magnusson's raider paid for his keep in his first season, which is all you can ask of a juvenile.

4th Aug KEMPTON
Won by **Treat Me Wild** (Loup Savage—Goes A Treat)
Foaled on 3rd April
Trained by R. Hannon—ridden by R. Smith

Only a tiny filly, Treat Me Wild delighted connections at the first time of asking at Bath over the minimum trip in April, and this surprising (14/1) victory would have added plenty of icing to a tasty little cake. The fact she beat The Crooked Ring speaks volumes for the filly, albeit that the David Evans' raider was giving lumps of weight away to the winner, and was only caught on the line. Treat Me Wild showed little for the rest of the season, and had been beaten plenty far enough in three all-weather efforts on sand late last year. It could just be that, unless the filly fills out during the first part of 2005, we might have seen the best of her already in racing terms.

4th Aug NEWCASTLE
Won by **Lady Misha** (Mister Baileys—Hakone)
Foaled on 26th January
Trained by Jedd O'Keefe—ridden by J. Mackay

Having secured a place in her previous race at Beverley over the same seven furlong trip, Lady Misha went on to finish second at Newcastle on soft ground over a mile, after this victory. It's difficult to write off the winner, as she is from Mister Bailey's stock who will run their respective hearts out for connections, though it has to be noted that this was one of the weaker Nursery races of the season. Lady Misha had shown very little in her first three outings, but, like her sire, produced better form when the distances were extended. She was far from disgraced over a mile in a half decent event at Ayr in October and it is far too early to write her off as an ordinary type just yet.

5th Aug CHEPSTOW
Won by **Dove Cottage** (Great Commotion—Pooka)
Foaled on 3rd April
Trained by W. Kittow—ridden by D. Kinsella

A weak Nursery, if only because a very ordinary Richard Hannon raider (Godsend) was made an 8/11 favourite, which duly got turned over. The winner had failed to show much form in his first three races, other than finishing just five lengths adrift of The Crooked Ring in a Warwick maiden in June. The step up to six furlongs worked the oracle, however, and the April 3rd foal went on to run second over seven on soft going at York next time out. Although failing to gain a place in his last two outings over a mile, it's worth noting that Dove Cottage ran the useful Something Exciting to less than four lengths at Goodwood, and it's too early to write off the gelding.

5th Aug FOLKESTONE
Won by **Lisa Mona Lisa** (Desert Style—Amneris)
Foaled on 1st February
Trained by V. Smith—ridden by T. Durcan

The first five horses home (of six) were covered by just two lengths, and the major reason the filly prevailed was her battling qualities, which had also seen her home in two previous victories from four starts. Frankie Dettori's mount (6/4 favourite) came to head Lisa Mona Lisa inside the distance, but Ted Durcan got another run out of the winner to score by the minimum margin. Two further efforts over seven and eight furlongs failed to reward connections with another cheque however. All three victories were gained on good/firm ground.

6th Aug HAYDOCK
Won by **Baymist** (Mind Games—Milliscent)
Foaled on 20th January
Trained by M.W. Easterby—ridden by R. Ffrench

The 25/1 winner was scoring her second success in five outings, having finished unplaced in the other three efforts. She went on to contest two more races during the season without troubling the judge. Her two victories were gained on good and good-to-soft ground, and as a Mind Games individual, it was no surprise to see her contest six of her seven races over five furlongs, and the minimum trip is about as far as she wants to go I'll wager. She was beating a previous Nursery winner Make Us Flush here, albeit in receipt of ten pounds.

6th Aug NEWMARKET(JULY)
Won by **Mighty Empire** (Second Empire—Barnabus)
Foaled on 28th February
Trained by M. Tompkins—ridden by L. Dettori

Mighty Empire justified favouritism in a seven strong field and

Frankie always looked confident aboard the Mark Tompkins raider. From Slip Anchor stock, it was hardly surprising to find the Second Empire colt improving as he stepped up in trip, and his next effort when runner up in an eight furlong contest was even better than this striking performance. A little disappointing over the mile on his final outing, Mighty Empire could leave the form well behind as a three-year-old, which included his first three ordinary efforts between May and July.

8th Aug REDCAR
Won by **Claret And Amber** (Forzando—Artistic Licence)
Foaled on 19th February
Trained by R. Fahey—ridden by P. Hanagan

Claret And Amber followed up this victory by scoring over an extra (seventh) furlong at Chester on soft going next time out. One placed effort from three subsequent outings was not a bad return in a trio of warm events, and with a good debut effort (third, beaten by just one length) at Beverley in July, this was a thoroughly acceptable first season for the early (19th February) foal.

9th Aug WINDSOR
Won by **Tequila Sheila** (Raise A Grand—Hever Rosina)
Foaled on 19th April
Trained by K. Burke—ridden by K. Fallon

This was the second of Tequila Sheila's two victories from her first four races, the previous success being gained in a Hamilton maiden at the second time of asking. It was apparent that her two worst performances came on fast ground, and a little give in the ground appears to suit Karl Burke's youngster. Tequila Sheila was beaten by an aggregate of twenty lengths in the three races that followed this victory in better class, and this would appear to be her grade. It could just be that she responded well to Fallon's urgings, and that strong handling will be the key to any future success.

12th Aug CHEPSTOW
Won by **Persian Rock** (Namid—Cairo Lady)
Foaled on 15th March
Trained by J. Osborne—ridden by D. Holland

This was the third decent performance in a row, as Persian Rock had started his career with a placed effort at Doncaster first time up, before going on to score in an ordinary Windsor maiden. Jamie Osborne's Namid gelding failed to build on this success but, that said, Darryll Holland's mount was taking on some serious opposition at both Ascot and Doncaster. Well thought of earlier in the season (good entries), Persian Rock might not have realised all the dreams of the connections, but any owner would have been proud of the record in his five races of his debut season.

12th Aug HAYDOCK
Won by **Make Us Flush** (Mind Games—Pearls)
Foaled on 14th February
Trained by A. Berry—ridden by F. Norton

With racing abandoned at Beverley, the going was predictably heavy here at Haydock, and Make Us Flush had already shown that she could handle such conditions. Three victories and a placed effort was a decent return in her first season from a total of twelve outings. As a Mind Games filly, it's fair to assume that Make Us Flush will be kept for sprinting, if she is to stay in training as a three-year-old.

13th Aug CATTERICK
Won by **Rowan Lodge** (Indian Lodge—Tirol Hope)
Foaled on 30th April
Trained by M. Tompkins—ridden by N. Mackay

Although his form tailed off towards the end of the season, Rowan Lodge recorded this victory and three other placed efforts from his first seven runs. A seemingly genuine type, Rowan Lodge ran well on all kinds of surfaces, and this victory was gained on soft ground. The winner was giving weight away to all bar one in the field (carried 9–4) and this was a thoroughly decent effort in beating a Richard Fahey raider (Favouring) by a neck, conceding plenty of weight in the process. Rowan Lodge was a winner of two events during the season, whilst claiming three placed positions in his other seven events. The dam was placed in Listed company at three, so connections have reason to be hopeful for the 2005 season. The fact that the two successes were gained at such different courses as Brighton and Catterick also bodes well for the future.

14th Aug NEWMARKET(JULY)
Won by **Nova Tor** (Trans Island—Nordic Living)
Foaled on 24th April
Trained by N. Littmoden—ridden by I. Mongan

Nova Tor won at the first time of asking on sand at Southwell, and went on to secure three further victories from twelve outings on turf, though Nick Littmoden's raider failed to make the frame in any of the other nine events. The good-to-soft conditions seemed to suit the Trans Island filly, who had previously scored on good ground. This 33/1 success was gained via Ian Mongan using forcing tactics, and it's worth noting that each of her three victories on turf was gained fairly comfortably, once she had got her head in front of the opposition. Fast ground did not seem to suit Nova Tor, as the filly finished nearer last than first on all five occasions that the ground was riding on the firm side of good.

16th Aug NOTTINGHAM
Won by **Coleorton Dancer** (Danehill Dancer—Tayovullin)
Foaled on 2nd April
Trained by K. Ryan—ridden by A. Mullen

This was the second of four victories on the bounce for the Danehill Dancer gelding, and Kevin Ryan's raider was justifying favouritism in no uncertain fashion here. Despite being raised from a lowly mark of 65 to 71, Coleorton Dancer was on the way to an eventual figure of 89, and connections are to be congratulated for the handling of the juvenile. Racing on going firmer than good on just the one occasion (disappointingly), Coleorton Dancer showed all the qualities of his successful sire by winning his four races by an aggregate of ten lengths, before running well down the field in his last two races when considerably raised in class. His first five efforts (including one on sand at Southwell) indicated little of what was to come, but he raced freely in his opening races, which could be the reason for such a transformation in his performances.

17th Aug YORK
Won by **Space Shuttle** (Makbul—Sky Music)
Foaled on 22nd March
Trained by T. Easterby—ridden by K. Fallon

This was a very decent Nursery event, and Space Shuttle responded positively to all of Fallon's urgings from the saddle close to home. Scoring by half a length and a length from decent types such as Distinctly Game and The Crooked Ring, Space Shuttle had the rest of the field well strung out on this good ground, and it was no surprise to see Tim Easterby's colt follow up in a Listed event at Ripon, albeit that he was sent off at a surprisingly generous price of 12/1 on that occasion.

Having scored on good-to-firm ground at Doncaster earlier in the season (on his third attempt), the Listed success was gained on good-to-soft ground, which indicates that this is a thoroughly genuine type, especially as Space Shuttle also recorded three placed efforts in his other six races. Beaten by an aggregate of only three and a half lengths in those races, Space Shuttle can be classed as a very pleasing type, despite the fact that he ran well down the field when considerably upped in class on his final effort at Doncaster in October.

19th Aug CHESTER
Won by **Coleorton Dancer** (Danehill Dancer—Tayovullin)
Foaled on 2nd April
Trained by K. Ryan—ridden by A. Mullen

The Danehill Dancer gelding was winning her third race in the space of just ten days, whilst another victory was to be gained at Newmarket just ten days later.

19th Aug YORK
Won by **Merchant** (Tagula—Easy Pop)
Foaled on 6th March
Trained by M. Bell—ridden by R. Mullen

Merchant was turned out here having won his maiden just two days before, and Michael Bell's raider fairly scorched home in the style of a decent horse. Perfectly at home on easy ground, Merchant went on to secure two more victories in a fine first season, reaching an official mark of 99 in the process.

20th Aug CHESTER
Won by **Claret And Amber** (Forzando—Artistic Licence)
Foaled on 19th February
Trained by R. Fahey—ridden by T. Hamilton

The winner was following up another handicap victory at

Redcar on firm ground and was showing his versatility by treating this field with contempt on soft going. Three unplaced efforts in warm company later in the season should not be held against the Forzando gelding.

20th Aug SALISBURY
Won by **Caly Dancer** (Entrepreneur—Mountain Dancer)
Foaled on 17th February
Trained by D. Elsworth—ridden by J. Fortune

Caly Dancer came into this race on the back of three placed efforts, after failing to trouble the judge on his first two outings. His previous run to this was also in a Nursery event, when finishing third behind King Of Blues at Newbury. David Elsworth loves training winners at Salisbury, his local track, and Caly Dancer won in the style of a decent horse as the first two home pulled well clear of their rivals, despite the winner being returned as one of the 6/1 co favourites in what had looked a tight contest on paper! The Entrepreneur gelding was beaten by ten lengths when finishing fifth in his final outing of the season over a mile, though David's representative will surely stay the eight furlongs (and possibly more) as a three-year-old.

20th Aug SANDOWN
Won by **Countdown** (Pivotal—Quiz Time)
Foaled on 2nd March
Trained by Sir M. Prescott—ridden by S. Sanders

Countdown was sold for 40,000 guineas out of Sir Mark Prescott's yard, after finishing second in another Nursery event at Windsor following this victory. The Pivotal colt had scored at Haydock immediately prior to contesting this event after finishing last of three (11/8 fav) at Hamilton on his debut.

21st Aug SANDOWN
Won by **Im Spartacus** (Namaqualand—Captivating)
Foaled on 16th April
Trained by I. Wood—ridden by M. Fenton

It was no surprise to see the winner returned at 20/1, as Ian Wood's raider had failed to trouble the judge in his previous six races. There had previously been plenty of optimism about the gelding, however, as he had taken a weak race at Brighton having run second at Bath at the start of April. Im Spartacus followed this Sandown victory by running down the field in two races when upped in class before claiming another toteplacepot position on good ground at Windsor in October. This leggy individual has worn blinkers and/or cheekpieces on most of his more recent outings. Having been campaigned throughout the winter season, Im Spartacus will need a rest at some stage! Now with David Flood.

23rd Aug WINDSOR
Won by **Key Secret** (Whittingham—Foxkey)
Foaled on 3rd March
Trained by M. Bell—ridden by Hayley Turner

Key Secret was winning her fourth race of the year, and though unsighted in three further races, Michael Bell's raider had more than paid her way for the season.

Key Secret started her career with a victory at Wolverhampton before notching an immediate hat trick, scoring at Leicester and York. Beaten by an aggregate of just six lengths thereafter in two further events when upped in class, Michael Bell eased the filly back down to this winning grade, and Key Secret slammed previous winner Countdown by five lengths in no uncertain fashion. Three more unplaced efforts closed the season, but these were in warm events, and the filly could return to winning ways when dropped back down in class. She has wandered about the racecourse on occasions, though there is nothing ungenuine about her at all.

24th Aug YARMOUTH
Marcela Zabala (Zaha—Bay Bianca)
Foaled on 11th March
Trained by J. Given—ridden by J. Fanning

This was only a modest Nursery event at best, and the winner was scoring off an official mark of just fifty-four, rising eventually to a maximum of fifty-eight. Having ran unplaced at Southwell first time up, Marcela Zabala scored on good to firm ground at Leicester on her turf debut, and won this race on soft ground; hence nobody can accuse the filly of being anything but genuine. James Given *upped the ante* by contesting two decent races with the Zaha filly after this victory, and whilst she was not totally outclassed, this is very much her mark I would suggest.

26th Aug MUSSELBURGH
Won by **Monashee Rose** (Monashee Mountain—Thorn Tree)
Foaled on 14th February
Trained by J.S. Moore—ridden by N. Mackay

Monashee Rose followed an unplaced effort first time up at Sandown with two victories. Following a comfortable victory at Carlisle, the filly showed battling qualities by winning this tale of heads and necks, as the first four horses home were separated by less than a length. Monashee Rose went on to contest another Nursery when finishing second at Bath, before disappointing connections with three unplaced efforts which closed her season. Likely to be kept for sprinting, Zafonic features in her bloodline and there are plenty of small races to be won with the filly.

27th Aug GOODWOOD
Won by **Miss Cassia** (Compton Place—Miller's Melody)
Foaled on 14th February
Trained by R. Hannon—ridden by R.L. Moore

The winner has been sold to race in the USA. Miss Cassia won her Nursery at the fifth time of asking, having claimed a runner-up position at Lingfield (turf) after finishing third of eight first time up at Newmarket. She followed this winning effort with two unplaced runs when considerably raised in class.

27th Aug NEWMARKET(JULY)
Won by **Merchant** (Tagula—Easy Pop)
Foaled on 6th March
Trained by M. Bell—ridden by Hayley Turner

Merchant justified odds of 8/11 when claiming this weak Nursery event before moving on to better things. The Tagula colt eventually went on to contest the Gran Criterium at Milan when finishing a creditable fourth in that Group 1 event. This was his third victory on the spin having won another Nursery the previous week at York, and with Hayley Turner reducing the burden via her claim, Merchant was effectively running off the same mark. Watch for similar moves this season from his shrewd trainer. Merchant won his next race at Newbury when landing the odds again, before being sold on late last year.

28th Aug NEWMARKET (JULY)
Won by **Coleorton Dancer** (Danehill Dancer—Tayovullin)
Foaled on 2nd April
Trained by K. Ryan—ridden by N. Callan

As mentioned earlier, Coleorton Dancer was winning his fourth race on the spin here, having secured two victories each on good and good-to-soft ground. Not disgraced in two further outings later in the season, Kevin Ryan's progressive type remains an interesting individual for 2005.

29th Aug BEVERLEY
Won by **Nufoos** (Zafonic—Desert Lynx)
Foaled on 4th February
Trained by M. Johnston—ridden by R. Hills

Nufoos was a typical Mark Johnston juvenile, tough and genuine, and game as a pebble, whatever that means! The winner had started her career with a decent placed effort at York, before justifying odds of 5/6 at Leicester on good-to-firm ground. Having contested Listed and Group 2 company in her next two outings, the filly responded positively to dropping down to this grade and ran out a facile winner, literally sprinting away from her opponents inside the final furlong. Going on to finish second to two decent types in closing her first season, Nufoos should be kept on the right side if she trains on.

30th Aug CHEPSTOW
Won by **Our Fugitive** (Titus Livius—Mystical Jumbo)
Foaled on 12th April
Trained by A. Carroll—ridden by D. Holland

Our Fugitive ran prominently throughout his six races as a juvenile, and connections should be happy with the Titus Livius colt who secured this victory and three placed efforts from July through to October. Showing little in his first two races, Our Fugitive indicated what was to come when finishing third at 50/1 at Windsor, which witnessed the start of some impressive efforts, culminating with a narrow defeat at the hands of Ingleton at Newmarket on soft ground, which can be classed as very useful form. The colt could well win some half decent prizes if remaining in training.

30th Aug NEWCASTLE
Won by **Night Of Joy** (King's Best—Gilah)
Foaled on 5th February
Trained by M. Jarvis—ridden by P. Robinson

A lengthy filly, Night Of Joy was winning her second race in succession here following the beating she handed out to seventeen rivals at Nottingham earlier in the month. Both of these victories were gained on ground with plenty of give, and it's worth noting that she ran down the field in her four other efforts during the season, on firmer ground. Night Of Joy failed to cope with classier rivals in two efforts following this victory, but she should not be dismissed on account of those two efforts. Michael Jarvis did not overrace the filly, and as an early foal (February 5th), she will win her fair share of prize money as a three-year-old I'll wager.

30th Aug WARWICK
Won by **Simplify** (Fasliyev—Simplicity)
Foaled on 2nd February
Trained by D. Loder—ridden by K. Darley

Being gelded at an early age didn't seem to have the desired effect on Simplify, and it's worth noting that the Fasliyev gelding was sold out of David Loder's stable, probably because of his dodgy attitude.

31st Aug RIPON
Won by **Breaking Shadow** (Danehill Dancer—Crimborne)
Foaled on 24th May
Trained by R. Fahey—ridden by P. Hanagan

As a half brother to several winners, Breaking Shadow was expected to win as a juvenile, and the Danehill Dancer gelding did not let connections down. Having been placed in two of his first three efforts prior to contesting this event, he went on to contest four other races without troubling the judge, before claiming the final Nursery on the last day of the season at Doncaster. There is little doubt that the winner prefers some ease in the ground, whilst the trainer again takes the plaudits for placing his horses so well.

2nd Sept CARLISLE
Won by **Kingsgate Bay** (Desert Sun—Selkirk Flyer)
Foaled on 12th March
Trained by J. Best—ridden by N. Pollard

John Best's raider has been sold to the USA after some decent efforts last term. John saddled the horse three times before gaining this victory (once on sand), whilst it's worth reporting from a trainer watch perspective, that the Maidstone based handler claimed three more victories with the gelding soon after the winter season at Lingfield began.

2nd Sept REDCAR
Won by **Caitlin** (Intikhab—Esteraad)
Foaled on 18th March
Trained by B. Smart—ridden by F. Lynch

The winner is reportedly dead unfortunately. Caitlin was Bryan Smart's one winner from eighteen Nursery representatives during the course of the season, and only prevailed in a finish of heads, as the first six horses home were covered by little more than two lengths. From a trainer's perspective, it's worth noting that Smart had saddled the filly four times at Southwell prior to contesting this event, though she had made her debut when running down the field at Pontefract back in April. Bryan then sent the youngster to contest another Nursery at Musselburgh, where she ran third in a field of eight, before going one step too far when taking on warm opposition at Newmarket where she was pulled up, presumably where a fatal injury occurred.

4th Sept HAYDOCK
Won by **Spaced** (Indian Rocket—Tolomena)
Foaled on 4th April
Trained by R. Hannon—R. Hughes

Spaced contested the last of his five efforts to date in this event, and connections must have been happy with the Indian Rocket colt, having secured two victories and a placed effort during the course of the season. Not seen on the racecourse until the back end of May, Spaced quickly made up for two unplaced efforts at Kempton and Lingfield (turf) by winning his maiden at Folkestone on good-to-soft ground. Richard Hannon's representative then contested his first Nursery event when running the useful Merchant to seven lengths before claiming this prize. With Tolomeo in the bloodline, Spaced should have no trouble staying ten furlongs and more as a three-year-old, and if anyone can find an opening for a decent race it is Richard Hannon.

5th Sept YORK
Won by **Diamonds And Dust** (Mister Baileys—Dusty Shoes)
Foaled on 5th February
Trained by M. Tompkins—ridden by P. Robinson

As a winner of a seven furlong race as a juvenile, Mark Tompkins will no doubt waste little time in finding out if this particular Mister Baileys colt gets the mile, a trip which can produce so many decent cheques for three-year-olds. The juvenile was brought back to contest a six furlong event at the end of the season, which is a little worrying, though soft ground could have been the reason for that decision by the trainer. The ground was good-to-firm for this victory, and there was much to like about his attitude when running on well under 9–5 to treat the opposition with a fair degree of contempt. Diamonds And Dust only claimed one other toteplacepot position from five starts during the campaign, but it's worth noting that he was only beaten by an aggregate of thirteen lengths in those races, and I predict there is plenty more to come from this fellow.

6th Sept BATH
Won by **Clinet** (Docksider—Oiche Mhaith)
Foaled on 5th April
Trained by P. Phelan—ridden by J. Egan

Clinet will always have problems winning races because of the way she starts her races, and this victory can (respectfully) be attributed to the lack of decent opposition as much as anything else. Struggling to keep up with the pace fully half a mile from home, Clinet was somehow able to thread her way through the twelve strong field to claim gold close to home, and there was precious little wrong with the way she went about her business when daylight appeared. She went on to claim her second placed effort of the season at Nottingham in another Nursery from her eighth race on turf, but this is very much her grade, and the Docksider filly might struggle as a three-year-old if kept in training.

6th Sept WARWICK
Won by **Viking Spirit** (Mind Games—Dane Dancing)
Foaled on 12th February
Trained by P. Harris—ridden by D. Holland

I presume that Walter Swinburn will take over the handling of this colt, who rewarded connections handsomely in his first season. Viking Spirit went on to claim his next race (another Nursery) at Nottingham before finishing down the field at Newmarket when the Mind Games colt looked to have gone over the top. Having scored on ground either side of good, Viking Spirit appears to be an admirable type, who gained two placed positions from his first three outings of the season prior to contesting this event. From Danehill stock, Viking Spirit looks sure to figure amongst Walter's winners in 2005.

7th Sept CATTERICK
Won by **Melandre** (Lujain—Talighta)
Foaled on 30th January
Trained by M. Brittain—ridden by T. Williams

A half decent type, it's worth noting that Mel Brittain resisted the temptation to run this filly on sand during the course of the season, which bodes well for her future, as the trainer clearly holds her in high regard, albeit (respectfully) in fairly ordinary events. Drawn in stall seven, Williams was able to use Melandre's initial burst of speed to good effect to secure a useful position before striking for home on this sharp track. Usually racing up with the pace in her races, Melandre was kept to the minimum trip in all seven of her races, where she also claimed a toteplacepot position in her next outing at Ripon in another Nursery event. Unplaced in her other five races during her first campaign (including her first four events), Melandre will not take racing by storm as a three-year-old, though I'll wager her canny trainer will find a little race somewhere in the calendar for this nice type to score. She was not beaten too far in any of her races as a juvenile, and may produce her best form on a sound surface in 2005.

7th Sept LEICESTER
Won by **Amphitheatre** (Titus Livius)
Foaled on 26th April
Trained by R. Johnson Houghton—ridden by L. Dettori

A fidgety type of individual, Amphitheatre is a half brother to three winners and might turn out to be a decent three-year-old if learning to settle down before contesting his events. This victory was gained on the last of his six races on turf (placed in one of his two starts on sand), having secured two placed efforts earlier in the season at Newmarket and York. The fact that those efforts were run at top class venues should not disguise the fact that this victory was gained in selling grade, and the races at Newmarket and York were class E events. That said, Frankie conjured a decent run from the juvenile to reverse form with the third horse home (Lorna Dune—the other joint favourite ridden by Fallon), and it is not beyond the realm of possibilities that the Titus Livius gelding could secure a small race as a three-year-old.

7th Sept LINGFIELD
Won by **Mitraillette** (Miswaki—Crockadore)
Foaled on 20th February
Trained by Sir M. Stoute—ridden by N. Mackay

Try not to get carried away with the fact this was a Michael Stoute winner, as there is every chance that she is a fairly ordinary type by the trainer's high standards. The handicapper had little chance to come to terms with the winner as this was just her fourth run of the season, though there is no denying that the filly won well enough in the end, beating nineteen rivals in the process to justify favouritism at the generous odds of 7/1. From Nijinsky stock, Mitraillette can only come on as a result of this final run of the 2004 campaign, and she was only beaten by an aggregate of twelve and a half lengths from her three unplaced efforts prior to this contest. Mitraillette should also improve for a step up in trip.

8th Sept DONCASTER
Won by **Swan Nebula** (Seeking The Gold—Bright Tiara)
Foaled on 15th February
Trained by Saeed Bin Suroor—ridden by L. Dettori

Unless Swan Nebula was over the top when she ran on soft going on her final outing of the season, I suggest that she will always be better on a sound surface, as was the case here at Doncaster when accounting for a half decent field, which included no less than twenty opponents. Swan Nebula broke the track record, though before reaching for your little black books, I should inform you that this is the only race of the season that is run at this distance on Town Moor. That aside, you could not help but be impressed by the winner who had shown a level of potential when lining up here at the same venue on her debut when finishing third of eight back in June. After an unplaced effort at Newbury, she returned to the Berkshire venue to win her maiden on good-to-firm ground a few weeks later. There was a break of five weeks before connections saddled the filly for this victory, and there is surely more success earmarked for Swan Nebula in 2005.

9th Sept DONCASTER
Won by **Singhalese** (Singspiel—Baize)
Foaled on 3rd March
Trained by J. Osborne—ridden by S. Drowne

A particularly good mover for a tall filly, Singhalese is a half sister to three winners and was not scoring out of turn, despite her starting price of 20/1 on this occasion. She contested this race on the back of two placed efforts at Nottingham and Newmarket, having finished unplaced (though only beaten four lengths) on her debut at Doncaster over seven furlongs on a good-to-firm surface. This was her fourth and final run of the season, and I'll wager that Jamie Osborne thinks a fair bit of this Singspiel filly. Prize money of over £20,000 from just four starts is not to be sniffed at, and I believe there will be more cheques to be won by Singhalese if she is kept in training. Eight to ten furlongs might turn out to be her optimum range of distances.

9th Sept EPSOM
Won by **Yajbill** (Royal Applause—Tee Cee)
Foaled on 23rd February
Trained by M. Channon—ridden by J. Quinn

A typically tenacious front runner from the Mick Channon yard, Yajbill was visored for his last four outings of the season, though, in fairness, there was precious little wrong with his first four attempts on the racecourse, having secured place prize money in three of those events. Mick knows this game inside out, and the move was immediately rewarded with a victory at Brighton before contesting this contest. The Royal Applause colt went on to complete the hat trick at Salisbury twenty days later, before running the useful Moth Ball to less than five lengths in a Listed event at Goodwood on his final start of the campaign. Reportedly an idle and lazy type, I wouldn't mind having half a dozen of the likes of Yajbill, whilst it's worth noting in closing that he has only been asked to run on good-to-soft or faster ground at the time of writing. His five-length demolition of the second horse home on this occasion at Epsom was gained on good-to-firm ground, which probably brings out the best in him.

11th Sept DONCASTER
Won by **Malinsa Blue** (Desert Style—Talina's Law)
Foaled on 29th March
Trained by J. Glover—ridden by F. Norton

Malinsa Blue was not winning out of turn, having finished second in three of her five races prior to this event. Malinsa Blue went on to run down the field on her final outing, but she had earned her winter rest by then.

11th Sept CHESTER
Won by **Comic Strip** (Marju—Comic)
Foaled on 7th May
Trained by Sir M. Prescott—ridden by M. Hills

A half sister to a useful US type, Comic Strip could literally be anything, and in the hands of Sir Mark Prescott could go on to secure some very decent events in 2005. After her debut victory by four lengths at Southwell, Comic Strip finished unplaced at Beverley on good-to-soft ground, and it could be that a sounder surface will ultimately turn out to be her preferred conditions. Comic Strip proceeded to win her final four races of the season, the first of which was gained in this contest on good ground. Her shortest winning margin was then gained next time out with plenty of ease in the ground, before trouncing the opposition on two further occasions when meeting with ideal conditions. Progressive is the word with a capital 'P' I would suggest, and the sky could be the limit for this filly, though with his feet firmly on the ground as always, Sir Mark will no doubt have handicaps in mind for this youngster. It's a sobering thought that, at the time of writing, Sir Mark Prescott has yet to saddle a British Classic contender!

11th Sept MUSSELBURGH
Won by **Succession** (Groom Dancer—Pitcroy)
Foaled on 16th March
Trained by Sir M. Prescott—ridden by J. Mackay

Another Mark Prescott raider to scrutinise, though I'm not 100% sure that this filly is genuine; I guess we should give her the benefit of doubt until we see her perform as a three-year-old. Whatever she is, Succession appears to hold a preference for decent ground, as was the case with this victory on her handicap debut. The Groom Dancer filly turned the race into something of a procession in all honesty, though she was not beating the strongest line up in the world in the process. She went on to complete her Nursery hat trick with victories at Yarmouth and Musselburgh, though they were generally there for the taking, and it is her effort behind Something Exciting at Goodwood in September that raises the question about her attitude. Succession finished third on that occasion, having been installed as the 3/1 favourite to land the event, though, like all fillies, she might simply have gone over the top I guess. She showed little of what was to come in her first four maiden races, but was expertly placed to notch her victories, as is usually the case with Sir Mark Prescott's raiders.

12th Sept GOODWOOD
Won by **Cyclical** (Pivotal—Entwine)
Foaled on 9th February
Trained by G. Butler—ridden by L. Dettori

Cyclical defied a burden of 9–7 here to win in the style of a very useful horse, though she failed to score in two subsequent races, albeit that they were warm events. Cyclical opened her account at the first time of asking at Hamilton in August, and it's something of a surprise that she was held back that long being a February 9th foal. I am not sure if there is a story behind that statistic, though all will be revealed in time I suppose. CYCLICAL is related to two useful types via Feet So Fast and Soar, and both horses were hugely impressive winners of several good juvenile events. Feet So Fast went on to score a brilliant hat trick as a three-year-old culminating with a victory in Ascot's Shergar Cup (also won as a juvenile), whilst Soar won both the Lowther and the Princess Margaret and was runner up in the Queen Mary last season. She failed to act on soft ground in the Cheveley Park but is still a filly with enormous potential. If Cyclical turns out to be half as good as a three-year-old, connections are in for a great season. Six furlongs could well be her optimum trip.

13th Sept BATH
Won by **Arbors Little Girl** (Paris House—Arbor Ealis)
Foaled on 4th February
Trained by B. Millman—ridden by A. Daly

Arbors Little Girl enjoyed a decent turf season last year, before going on to disappoint connections a little in a winter campaign on sand. I was also a little surprised that the Paris House filly contested races at a mile on the all weather surfaces. I would have thought that seven furlongs was as far as she might want to travel at full speed, though she might toughen up as a three-year-old to get the mile. Either way, she took this race by the scruff of the neck and the result was beyond any doubt some way from home. Beating another Nursery winner in the process, this wasn't bad form, coming off the back of a hard fought victory at Bath on her debut. Although unplaced in her final two starts on turf, she was beaten less than nine lengths on aggregate, and there could be more prize money to be won when tackling turf again in 2005.

13th Sept MUSSELBURGH won by **Oceanico Dot Com**
(Hernando—Karen Blixen)
Foaled on 12th February
Trained by A. Berry—ridden by F. Norton

Alan Berry likes his sprinters, and this nippy type might be aimed at a maximum of six furlongs early in 2005. Although receiving plenty of weight, there was plenty to like about this performance, and a total of two victories and two placed efforts from eight races on turf will have pleased connections. Placed either side of her first victory at Ripon on good-to-soft ground, varying conditions do not seem to bother this Hernando filly, though she was beaten a long way when last of thirteen on sand two days in to the winter season.

13th Sept REDCAR
Won by **Connotation** (Mujahid—Seven Wonders)
Foaled on 12th February
Trained by P. D'Arcy—ridden by L. Dettori

This well bred filly was beating something of a talking horse (Clove) from the Barry Hills yard when capturing this prize, so it must have come as something of a disappointment to connections when she failed to cope with the slight rise in class when finishing unplaced at 'headquarters' next time out. Connotation was then saddled for a winter campaign, and I just hope that we haven't already seen the best of what might still be an interesting filly. Connotation had shown that she could cope with the undulations at Brighton on firm ground at the first time of asking, which is no mean feat in itself. Finishing second that day, she followed that effort up with another decent effort on the Polytrack surface at Lingfield before disappointing at the same venue over seven furlongs.

14th Sept SALISBURY
Won by **Something Exciting** (Halling—Faraway Waters)
Foaled on 7th March
Trained by D. Elsworth—ridden by J. Fortune

Although eventually finishing a slightly disappointing second behind Squaw Dance in a Listed event towards the back end of the season, when starting as an even money favourite, Something Exciting had paid for her keep by notching a decent hat trick prior to contesting that final run of the season. This was the first of those three victories, which was gained on soft ground that seems to be the key to the Halling filly. If she takes after her sire as a three-year-old, David Elsworth will have a great deal to look forward to in the coming months, and will soon forget his experience at the Jockey Club headquarters! Something Exciting had shown little of what was to come in her first three unplaced outings, but all of those efforts were attempted on fast ground, and I think we are all a bit wiser now. Something Exciting went on to beat decent fields at Goodwood and Newmarket before the slight blip in October, and she remains a progressive filly in my eyes, despite that defeat.

14th Sept YARMOUTH
Won by **Succession** (Groom Dancer—Pitcroy)
Foaled on 16th March
Trained by Sir M. Prescott—ridden by S. Sanders

This was the middle leg of a handicap hat trick for Mark Prescott's progressive juvenile, and after the event the returned starting price of 9/4 looked particularly generous, despite the fact that Succession only had half a length to spare in the shadow of the post.

15th Sept BEVERLEY
Won by **Belton** (Lujain—Efficacious)
Foaled on 9th March
Trained by Ronald Thompson—Ridden by K. McEvoy

Racing is (thankfully) not all about high class pedigrees and Pims on a hot summer's day, and this selling Nursery event produced a great finish, albeit that the protagonists are all (respectfully) ordinary types. The starting price of 20/1 was hardly surprising, as the winner had shown little (or nothing) in his five outings, though Lujain representatives are always worth keeping an eye on in this grade. There might be another small race to be won with Belton, though two poor winter efforts on sand at the time of writing hardly inspire confidence.

16th Sept YARMOUTH
Won by **Rebel Rebel** (Revoque—French Quarter)
Foaled on 25th March
Trained by N. Callaghan—L. Dettori

Neville Callaghan considers the winner as a potentially serious three-year-old in the making. There was another victory to be gained after this, before Rebel Rebel finally had to give best in a warm event late in the season.

16th Sept YARMOUTH
Won by **Lorna Dune** (Desert Story—Autumn Affair)
Foaled on 21st February
Trained by J. O'Shea—ridden by D. Sweeney

Loma Dune had claimed two toteplacepot positions from five races on turf before landing this prize, though two subsequent races failed to produce any further prize money for connections. The filly raced exclusively at nine furlongs in the five winter races at the time of writing, securing just one placed effort in the process. Lorna Dune might have to revert to this winning trip of a mile to gain any further victories, though I wouldn't bet on that scenario actually occurring.

17th Sept AYR
Won by **Je Suis Belle** (Efisio—Blossom)
Foaled on 15th March
Trained by B. Hills—ridden by A. Culhane

I was a little surprised to learn that Je Suis Belle had been sent to Gay Kelleway for a future on sand, as Barry Hills had secured this victory and two other placed efforts from just five races on turf in 2004. A 50/1 chance on her debut at Windsor in July, the Efisio filly soon put her name on the scoreboard by reaching the frame in Goodwood and Pontefract maiden races before contesting this event, where she showed good battling qualities in winning a race where the first six horses home were separated by just one length! The fact that she failed to build on the success in a decent race at Newmarket afterwards fails to convince me that Guy Reed has done the right thing with this seemingly genuine filly.

17th Sept NOTTINGHAM
Won by **Viking Spirit** (Mind Games—Dane Dancing)
Foaled on 12th February
Trained by P. Harris—ridden by I. Mongan

It will be interesting to see how Walter Swinburn handles these Peter Harris runners, now that the trainer has retired. This was Viking Spirit's second win in the space of eleven days, and there should be more to come in 2005.

18th Sept AYR
Won by **Comic Strip** (Marju—Comic)
Foaled on 7th May
Trained by Sir M. Prescott—ridden by S. Sanders

This was the second Nursery victory for Sir Mark Prescott's juvenile who went on to lift serious prizes later in the season.

18th Sept CATTERICK
Won by **Secret Pact** (Lend A Hand—Schust Madame)
Foaled on 4th March
Trained by M. Johnston—ridden by R. Ffrench

Despite the fact that Secret Pact lost his 'tackle' in the close season, the operation is likely to make a man out of him, as so many of the Mark Johnston horses have proved down the years. A keen sort who likes to race up with the pace, Secret Pact could win his fair share of prize money in 2005, if his first year in racing is anything to go by. Placed in two of his first four starts (fourth of nine on his debut at Mussleburgh), Secret Pact won his maiden at Carlisle on firm ground before scoring here on a similar surface. The Lend A Hand gelding then went on to contest two decent Nursery events, and was placed in both of them, offering genuine hope for the 2005 campaign. Beaten less than three lengths in aggregate by Something Exciting and Alpine Gold in those races, one thing is for sure, Secret Pact will not be heading off the track for stud duties!

18th Sept WARWICK
Won by **Danehill Willy** (Danehill Dancer—Lowtown)
Foaled on 17th March
Trained by N. Callaghan—ridden by N De Souza

Having shown plenty of scope when an unfancied 10/1 chance on his debut (finished second of six at Yarmouth), Danehill Willy revealed that he had plenty of his sire's talent by claiming this event, before moving on to supplement the victory at Newmarket on soft ground, beating eleven opponents in the process. 'Willy' failed to trouble the judge on his other three outings during the course of the season, but his seventh place in a Listed event at Newmarket in October offers hope for the future. As a half brother to several winners, it would take a brave person to suggest that more prize money will not be won by this individual, albeit in secondary races in the main.

19th Sept HAMILTON
Won by **Windy Prospect** (Intikhab—Yellow Ribbon)
Foaled on 8th April
Trained by P. Blockley—ridden by M. Fenton

The problem with Paul Blockley winners is that you know, somewhere along the line, the horses in question will be aimed at the all weather courses, which I find frustrating. How are we meant to keep a hold on form lines when winning horses are being directed towards two-bob events? Paul is a master of the scenario I will concede, and yes, the argument is turned on its head here because Windy Prospect was winning this race AFTER scoring at Southwell! To be fair, the Intikhab colt had also won at Wolverhampton earlier in the season, and Windy Prospect might be a talented enough individual to have a decent future under both codes of flat racing.

20th Sept CHEPSTOW
Won by **Cree** (Indian Ridge—Nightitude)
Foaled on 12th March
Trained by W. Muir—ridden by S. Sanders

Cree was blinkered when gaining a place position early in his career (wore the blinds on three occasions) but the aid was dispensed with on his final six outings, during which time he scored this victory, whilst claiming two other toteplacepot positions. His best efforts have all come from easy ground, and it literally cannot be too heavy for most of the Indian Ridge stock.

20th Sept LEICESTER
Won by **Magical Romance** (Barathea—Shouk)
Foaled on 5th February
Trained by B. Meehan—R. Winston

Leicester will remain famous for at least one thing from the 2004 campaign, and that derives from the fact that the Cheveley Park winner won a Nursery race at the venue during the course of the season! Yes, it was here at Leicester that Brian Meehan's Magical Romance contested her one and only two-year-old handicap race, en route to securing the Group 1 prize at Newmarket ten days later. The Barathea filly had claimed her maiden at only the second time of asking at Kempton in July, but few (if any) pundits could have predicted that a three length victory over Aberdeen Girl (apologies to connections) would have been enough to lift the Newmarket spectacle! All three victories were gained on good/fast ground, and Magical Romance never raced on any other going during her first season. The fact that she was beaten thirteen lengths by Soar at Ascot in between her two victories is a great compliment to James Fanshawe's filly, though that will be of little comfort to James who had the form reversed so much against his filly at Newmarket. There is nothing to add to the tale, except to hope that you were on the 40/1 winner at 'headquarters'!

21st Sept NEWMARKET(RM)
Won by **Bunny Rabbit** (Cherokee Run—Jane's The Name)
Foaled on 24th February
Trained by B. Meehan—ridden by L. Dettori

Bunny Rabbit was one of three Nursery winners for Brian Meehan in the space of two days, and it's worth noting that the trainer failed to win another two-year-old handicap with twenty-four further raiders outside of this period. Although this event was nothing special, the winner scored off an official rating of 87 (reasonable mark) and was put away for the winter following this effort. Although failing to make the frame in four previous races (including one on Lingfield's Polytrack surface), Frankie's mount was unlucky in running at Doncaster prior to running here, and this victory was waiting to happen.

21st Sept NEWMARKET(RM)—**The Pheasant Flyer** (Prince Sabo—Don't Jump)
Foaled on 17th March
Trained by B. Meehan—ridden by J. Fortune

Another winner for Brian Meehan who was on a roll at the time, and The Pheasant Flyer was supplementing a maiden victory at Warwick on similar good-to-firm ground earlier in the month. The winner had one more run later in the year, but that contest was run on soft ground, and decent going could be the key to this Prince Sabo gelding.

22nd Sept LINGFIELD
Won by **Rebel Rebel** (Revoque—French Quarter)
Foaled on 25th March
Trained by N. Callaghan—O. Urbina

Rebel Rebel was winning his second handicap in the space of just six days, and trainer Neville Callaghan is adept at finding ways to make the most of a winning mark in such circumstances. Scoring at 4/5 in a field of twenty runners, his reputation came before him and a two length victory was predictable enough. The Revoque gelding went on to contest a really competitive Nursery at Ascot just four days later, but was unable to contain the challenge of Wise Dennis on that occasion, going down by the thick end of two lengths. Always racing in competitive events from day one, Rebel Rebel finished unplaced in his first four races before running into this impressive phase of form.

23rd Sept BRIGHTON
Won by **Moth Ball** (Royal Applause—Chrysalis)
Foaled on 3rd April
Trained by J. Osborne—ridden by D. Holland

This was the middle win of three for Moth Ball during the course of the season, culminating in a Listed victory at York, which saw the Royal Applause colt sold to America. It's worth noting that Darryll Holland rode the horse to win on every occasion, despite only sharing the eight races that the two-year-old contested with another jockey. Note the Osborn/Hellend raiders this term.

23rd Sept PONTEFRACT
Won by **Glorious Step** (Diesis—Bessie's Chips)
Foaled on 6th April
Trained by J. Gosden—ridden by J. Fortune

You ignore John Gosden's Nursery raiders at your peril, and this particular horse won off an official mark of 85 and could literally be anything as a three-year-old. A half sister to a decent US type, Glorious Step won this fillies-only event in the style of a progressive horse, and it's worth noting that the trainer had sent her over to France to contest a Group 3 event before coming on here to Ponte. Beaten by less than a length on her debut effort at Yarmouth, the Diesis filly went on to win her maiden at Windsor before crossing the water as previously mentioned. Glorious Step finished well down the field on heavy ground, and as she has won on firm and good-to-firm in her two victories, I will leave it up to you to deduce what might turn out to be her optimum conditions!

24th Sept HAYDOCK
Won by **Tagula Sunrise** (Tagula—Lady From Limerick)
Foaled on 22nd February
Trained by R. Fahey—ridden by P. Hanagan

Tagula Sunrise was justifying favouritism when winning this competitive fifteen runner handicap, and was yet another winner for Richard Fahey in this sector. The Tagula filly had been a model of consistency all season, securing a victory and five placed efforts from her previous seven starts. This was her first effort on ground anything other than fast, and she handled it with aplomb. A good moving type, however, quick ground is always likely to bring out the best in her and it will be interesting to see where she goes next. I just hope she is kept in training and moves on to better things.

25th Sept RIPON
Won by **Talcen Gwyn** (Fayruz—Cheerful Knight)
Foaled on 2nd May
Trained by M. F. Harris—ridden by A. Nicholls

Six of the first seven horses home were drawn in stalls ten to fifteen (inclusive) in a field of fifteen runners, so form your own conclusion! Although unsighted in ten other races during the year, Talcen Gwyn had at least won a small race at Brighton on his second start, and both victories were gained on fast ground.

26th Sept ASCOT
Won by **Wise Dennis** (Polar Falcon—Bowden Rose)
Foaled on 11th April
Trained by A. Jarvis—ridden by K. McEvoy

Alan Jarvis is (respectfully) regarded as a workmanlike trainer, but it's worth noting that the trainer has had some very useful horses in his yard down the years, and Wise Dennis could be another of them. The gelding was beating previous winner

Rebel Rebel in the style of a very useful horse here, and went on to run another good race when finishing second in a Listed event at Pontefract in his next (final) outing. There was little notice of what was to come earlier in the season, as Wise Dennis had managed to secure just one placed effort from four previous outings on turf before gaining this victory. As an April foal, there might be plenty more to come as a three-year-old.

26th Sept MUSSELBURGH
Won by **Succession** (Groom Dancer—Pitcroy)
Foaled on 16th March
Trained by Sir M. Prescott—ridden by D. Holland

Succession was building up quite a reputation by now, and was a typical Sir Mark Prescott improver when winning this event, before going on to run Something Exciting to less than three lengths at Goodwood in her final run of the season. This was her third handicap win on the bounce within the space of fifteen days; hence it's not difficult to deduce that she is a tough filly and no mistake.

27th Sept WINDSOR
Won by **Forzeen** (Forzando—Mazurkanova)
Foaled on 30th April
Trained by J. Osborne—ridden by E. Ahern

Jamie Osborne has already stated that his two-year-olds are a little behind schedule this season at the time of writing, so don't be too disheartened if his runners have not set the world alight by the time you read this publication. It's certainly worth noting his juveniles from this sire (Forzando) as they are typical of Jamie's best representatives, tough and genuine types who can take plenty of racing in their first year. The winner was sold to the US during the winter.

28th Sept NOTTINGHAM
Won by **Penalty Kick** (Montjeu—Dafrah)
Foaled on 11th April
Trained by N. Callaghan—ridden by K. Fallon

A potentially useful stayer in the making, Penalty Kick made his debut over seven furlongs, and it was no surprise to see him win this event, the first ten furlong Nursery of the season. The biggest problem that trainer Neville Callaghan might have with this individual is that he raced freely as a juvenile, though there is plenty of time for Neville and his team to correct that problem. Dropped back in trip after this victory, it's worth noting that Penalty Kick was beaten fair and square over a mile, and surely there is more to come over a distance of ground this term, especially on genuinely good ground, or preferably with a little juice in the surface. Kieren Fallon rode him to victory here and it's possible that strong handling will always be a requirement. His first three outings had produced nothing of note under tender handling, and the conclusion is fairly obvious.

30th Sept GOODWOOD
Won by **Something Exciting** (Halling—Faraway Waters)
Foaled on 7th March
Trained by D. Elsworth—ridden by T. Quinn

This was the middle victory during the course of a hat trick for the winner, and Something Exciting showed all the qualities of a decent three-year-old in the making.

30th Sept NEWMARKET(RM)
Won by **Obe Gold** (Namaqualand—Gagajulu)
Foaled on 26th March
Trained by M. Channon—ridden by A. Culhane

As tough as old boots, Obe Gold is a typical Mick Channon representative who was aimed at the competitive Redcar

Listed event just two days after this victory, and sure enough, the colt was up to the task when beating hotpot Caesar Beware. A winner from the wrong side of the draw here, Obe Gold had started his racing life in good order, winning one race and securing two places in his first four outings. The colt then went off the boil but was never beaten far in four further efforts, and 20/1 was a generous starting price here in the circumstances. A front runner that always seems to find a little more when coming under pressure, Obe Gold looks sure to win more races.

1st Oct LINGFIELD
Won by **Seasons Estates** (Mark Of Esteem—La Fazenda)
Foaled on 26th April
Trained by B. Millman—ridden by P. Doe

Mark Of Esteem was a decent miler, and it was no surprise to see Seasons Estates win this seven furlong event, having finished third over course and distance here prior to this victory. There was little to note about her three previous efforts, but the filly was beaten little more than twenty lengths on aggregate on those occasions; hence these last two decent efforts in wrapping up her season were not impossible to predict. Only an average juvenile, the winner is related to winners on the continent, so who knows where she might end up.

2nd Oct EPSOM
Won by **Louphole** (Loup Sauvage—Goodwood Lass)
Foaled on 4th April
Trained by P. Makin—ridden by D. Sweeney

Surely a sprinter through and through, Louphole was winning at Epsom having scored at another undulating track at Brighton earlier in the season. Both victories were gained on fast ground, and there should be more to come from this Loup

Sauvage gelding. Beaten less than four lengths on his first two starts (on aggregate), Louphole put in a couple of disappointing efforts before bouncing back to form when beaten just a length at Windsor just five days before this effort.

2nd Oct NEWMARKET(RM)
Won by **Wedding Party** (Groom Dancer—Ceanothus)
Foaled on 18th March
Trained by Mrs A. Perrett—ridden by J. Murtagh

Winning this fillies only Nursery, Wedding Party put distance between herself and her field, though it's worth noting that the other six horses all finished in a heap, separated by barely a length. Although the ground was officially classed as good, rain had made the ground very tacky, and it's worth noting that the Groom Dancer filly went on to run second in a Listed event at Newbury on heavy ground on her next outing. Finishing within five lengths of Magical Romance on her debut at Kempton on fast ground in July, Wedding Party is obviously a tough and genuine filly who looks set to build on an impressive first season.

4th Oct PONTEFRACT
Won by **Safendonseabiscuit** (Danzig Connection—The Fugative)
Foaled on 14th March
Trained by S. Kirk—ridden by M. Hills

Safendonseabiscuit has gone on to run too many times over the winter to assess properly for 2005, so let's just look at the way he was directed from day one. Placed in three of his eight starts before lifting this prize, it's worth noting that he finished close behind several winners in those efforts. The colt had only raced on fast ground before disappointing connections when finishing down the field in soft ground at Newmarket immediately following this victory.

4th Oct WINDSOR
Won by **Come On Jonny** (Desert King—Idle Fancy)
Foaled on 2nd May
Trained by R. Beckett—ridden by D. Holland

A half brother to three winners, Come On Jonny won on soft ground here and these conditions might be his optimum requirement in the months and years to come. Beaten only a length on his second start at Thirsk on good-to-soft ground, Come On Jonny went on to finish last of thirteen in a better race at Windsor after this victory, though fast conditions might not have suited the Desert King colt.

5th Oct CATTERICK
Won by **Hansomelle** (Titus Livius—Handsome Anna)
Foaled on 12th March
Trained by B. Mactaggart—ridden by Dale Gibson)

Hailing from Bigstone stock, a distance of ground should not inconvenience this filly and she was winning over this seven furlong trip at the first time of asking. She went on to finish third behind the useful Crosspeace on her last outing of the season at the same distance, having won her maiden over six at Hamilton on fast ground on her second start. To show Hansomelle in her true light, it's probably best to dwell on the fact that she was beaten by an aggregate of less than eleven lengths in her four defeats last term.

8th Oct YORK
Won by **Ingleton** (Komaite—Dash Cascade)
Foaled on 14th February
Trained by B. McMahon—ridden by G. Gibbons

This was the middle victory of three (on the bounce), having been beaten by an aggregate of just six lengths when finishing unplaced in his first two starts at Nottingham and York. The trainer had shown patience in not going back to the well too quickly after Ingleton had won in the style of a good horse when winning his maiden at Ayr on good-to-soft ground, and it is a compliment to the Komaite colt that all ground conditions seem to come alike to this likeable type. A horse that likes racing up with the pace, Ingleton is the type of jeuvenile you would love to own.

10th Oct BATH
Won by **Chilly Cracker** (Largesse—Polar Storm)
Foaled on 4th March
Trained by R. Hollinshead—ridden by D. Sweeney

It's always difficult to assess Reg Hollinshead's runners, because by definition they are ordinary types, but the trainer does have a knack of winning a race with them! Chilly Cracker was a typical representative from the yard and it's worth noting that the filly had been Reg's first juvenile runner of the season at Warwick back in April. She finished second that day after finding trouble in running, and this was a well-earned victory, and nobody denies the veteran trainer his share of victories.

10th Oct NEWCASTLE
Won by **Hows That** (Vettori—Royalty)
Foaled on 23rd March
Trained by K. Burke—ridden by Darren Williams

Only a winner of a moderate (selling) Nursery event, punters who latched on to the 6/1 favourite will not mind that comment at all. This was a typical Newcastle sprint, because the eighteen strong field split into two groups very quickly, and the form of these Gosforth Park races is questionable to say the least. There is no denying that the Vettori filly had given notice of a good run here, however, having been marginally beaten at Ripon on good-to-soft ground on her previous start.

10th Oct GOODWOOD
Won by **Enforcer** (Efisio—Tarneem)
Foaled on 16th April
Trained by W. Muir—ridden by R. Miles

Not many horses pass the entire field to come and win a sixteen runner event, but Enforcer finished with a fair old rattle here and could literally be anything in 2005.

11th Oct AYR
Won by **Paris Bell** (Paris House—Warning Bell)
Foaled on 24th March
Trained by T. Easterby—ridden by P. Quinn

Racing with plenty of juice in the ground in the main, Paris Bell was a useful performer in his first season, and was setting up a sequence of victories when scoring here in soft conditions. Unplaced in his previous six races, there was no surprise when a starting price of 33/1 was returned, and few could have predicted the incredible change in form for Tim Easterby's gelding. A leggy type that races up with the pace, Paris Bell is a half brother to several winners and will surely go on to secure further victories, especially when racing on his favoured ground.

11th Oct WINDSOR
Won by **Alright My Son** (Pennekam—Pink Stone)
Foaled on 5th March
Trained by R. Hannon—ridden by R.L. Moore

A consistent horse all season, Alright My Son thoroughly deserved his victory, having finished second to three useful types earlier in the season. The winner went on to run down the field on his final outing in a competitive handicap at Doncaster on soft ground, but better conditions might bring out the best in this fellow as a three-year-old. A distance of ground could bring about further victories.

12th Oct AYR
Won by **King's Account** (King Of Kings—Fighting Countess)
Foaled on 13th May
Trained by M. Johnston—ridden by K. Darley

A late foal, King's Account was typically robbed of his tackle by Mark Johnston and his team, but this should merely make the King Of Kings gelding concentrate on the job in hand, and there is no knowing where the horse could go from here. This was his final run of the season, having won his maiden on (opposite) good-to-firm ground at Beverley on his previous start. Three previous efforts had secured the runner up position on each occasion, and as the horse had started life contesting a seven furlong event, racing over a distance of ground as a three-year-old is on the cards in 2005.

14th Oct NEWMARKET(RM)
Won by **Danehill Willy** (Danehill Dancer—Lowtown)
Foaled on 17th March
Trained by N. Callaghan—ridden by D. Holland

A typical Danehill Dancer type, Danehill Willy was winning his second race in succession, having secured a seven furlong event at Warwick on good-to-soft ground. This victory was gained over a mile in softer conditions, before possibly going a step too far by contesting a ten furlong event at 'headquarters' on his final start of the season. There was no sign of staying potential earlier in the season, as Neville Callaghan had started the horse over five furlongs at Yarmouth, when Danehill Willy finished second on good ground. Two efforts down the field followed that initial outing, before the colt went on to win at Warwick.

15th Oct NEWMARKET(RM)
Won by **Ingleton** (Komaite—Dash Cascade)
Foaled on 14th February
Trained by B. McMahon—ridden by G. Gibbons

This was the last of three successive victories for McMahon's raider and the Komaite colt won this off an official rating of 84 and is progressing nicely.

16th Oct CATTERICK
Won by **Knock Bridge** (Rossini—Touraneena)
Foaled on 15th March
Trained by P.D. Evans—ridden by T. Queally

Knock Bridge was winning for the first time, having secured two placed positions from five efforts before contesting this seven furlong event. This victory was gained on good-to-soft ground, before the winner went on to contest the last Nursery race of the season where he finished down the field on similar going. The main factor to consider with this individual is that he tends to give ground away at the start, and it was possibly more a fact that the leading contenders did not run their respective races in this event that brought about the victory.

18th Oct PONTEFRACT
Won by **Toldo** (Tagula—Mystic Belle)
Foaled on 2nd May
Trained by G.M. Moore—ridden by L. Dettori

This was the last of three successive victories for George Moore's juvenile, and though some pundits have questioned the gelding's temperament, it's worth noting that the previous two victories were gained on successive days, so I'm not sure where these critics are coming from. Well beaten in his first five starts, Toldo turned things around when finishing second on soft ground at Catterick before setting up his winning sequence. Toldo went on to contest a decent handicap at Doncaster in similar conditions next time up, but was well and truly put in his place by the useful Crosspeace. As for those critics, it's worth pointing out that his three victories were gained on good, heavy and good-to-firm ground. A two-year-old can barely be any more genuine than that! As a late foal, Toldo could yet go on to better things, albeit in his own class.

22nd Oct DONCASTER
Won by **Alpine Gold** (Montjeu—Ski For Gold)
Foaled on 3rd May
Trained by J. Dunlop—ridden by I. Mongan

It's worth noting that John Dunlop also saddled the runner up in this event, so the stable was on something of a roll when the winner contested this race. Fair play to the Montjeu filly however, as she was gaining her second successive victory here, following her maiden win on similarly soft ground at Chepstow over the same (mile) trip as on her previous outing. The filly was unplaced in her other three starts, and the jury remains out regarding her future. In all fairness, she was contesting a warm Listed event at Newmarket on her final start, and was only beaten by six lengths when finishing sixth of seven to Squaw Dance.

22nd Oct NEWBURY
Won by **Moon Forest** (Woodborough—Ma Belle Luna)
Foaled on 2nd May
Trained by P. Chapple-Hyam—ridden by Thomas Yeung

The Woodborough colt was to the fore throughout in his two victories at Warwick and here at Newbury, and this well related type appears to be tough and genuine. Peter's raider has only raced on soft ground to date, starting well enough when marginally beaten in a Warwick maiden. As a late foal, Moon Forest could yet be anything, and is with a top trainer who will get the very best from this individual, who will surely produce his best form on soft ground.

23rd Oct DONCASTER
Won by **Crosspeace** (Cape Cross—Announcing Peace)
Foaled on 26th April
Trained by M. Johnston—ridden by R. Ffrench

Cape Cross was a very decent miler, and there is every chance that Crosspeace will follow in his footsteps. Starting over six furlongs on good ground at Newcastle, this colt was beaten by just a length before going on to score in his final two outings. Leading from trap to line over seven furlongs in testing ground here, Crosspeace was supplementing another decent victory at Newcastle in opposite (good-to-firm) conditions over a shorter trip. Mark Johnston is just the chap to get the best out of a colt that was winning from an official mark of 84, though that figure is sure to be improved upon in 2005.

23rd Oct NEWBURY
Won by **Paris Bell** (Paris House—Warning Bell)
Foaled on 24th March
Trained by T. Easterby—ridden by P. Quinn

This was the middle of the gelding's three victories late in the season, and Tim Easterby's raider had this field well and truly strung out some way from home, winning in the style of a very promising type. Paris Bell went on to notch his hat trick when winning another handicap at Catterick in November.

27th Oct YARMOUTH
Won by **Russian Rocket** (Indian Rocket—Soviet Girl)
Foaled on 27th April
Trained by Mrs C. Dunnett—ridden by Hayley Turner

Quite a late foal, Russian Rocket was a fairly small juvenile and did well to win a race in all honesty. Unplaced in his first two races, Russian Rocket finished second in his next two outings before running down the field in the hot Redcar Listed event prior to contesting this event on soft ground. Easy ground could bring about further success for connections.

1st Nov REDCAR
Won by **The Pen** (Lake Coniston—Come To The Point)
Foaled on 11th April
Trained by P. Haslam—ridden by N. Pollard

These late Nursery events are difficult to win, not because of the class of opposition, but through the sheer number of horses in the respective races. Nineteen hopefuls lined up for this event, and Pat Haslam's raider was winning her second race in three attempts after an ordinary effort on his debut back in July. The two victories were gained on opposite types of ground; hence it is fair to suggest that this Lake Coniston filly is a tough and reliable sort. The impressive part about this victory was that Pollard's mount was able to overcome a seemingly poor draw, as The Pen was the only horse from a single figure stall to finish in the first seven positions.

2nd Nov CATTERICK
Won by **Paris Bell** (Paris House—Warning Bell)
Foaled on 24th March
Trained by T. Easterby—ridden by P. Quinn

The last victory of the three races mentioned earlier in despatches. Paris Bell moved his official mark from 62 to 75 in the space of just three weeks.

4th Nov NOTTINGHAM
Won by **Penang Sapphire** (Spectrum—Penang Pearl)
Foaled on 11th April
Trained by G. Butler—ridden by C. Catlin

Not inconvenienced by easy ground, Penang Sapphire scored at odds of 40/1 after two previous efforts had brought about defeats by an aggregate of over thirty lengths. Gerard Butler's raider had also performed poorly on two all weather efforts at the time of writing.

5th Nov YARMOUTH
Won by **Bowled Out** (Dansili—Braissim)
Foaled on 3rd May
Trained by P. McBride—ridden by T. Queally

Another late season outsider to prevail, Bowled Out belied odds of 25/1 to score in decent style, though, winning off an official mark of 60, this might not have been the most competitive of events, despite the fact that twenty runners faced the starter. The first four horses home all came from high figures in the draw, which might have been another significant factor. The Dansili filly obviously appreciated easy ground as three previous races had given no indication whatsoever of what might happen here.

6th Nov DONCASTER
Won by **Breaking Shadow** (Danehill Dancer—Crimbourne)
Foaled on 24th May
Trained by R. Fahey—ridden by P. Hanagan

This victory won Richard Fahey the Nursery crown as far as trainers are concerned, even though the likes of Sir Mark Prescott and David Elsworth were well clear of Richard from a percentage perspective in 2004. The winner had scored on similar good-to-soft ground at Ripon in August over six furlongs, though this victory over a slightly longer trip bodes well for the future.

BREEDING AND THE IMPORTANCE OF FOALING DATES

I made the point in the opening chapter that the last four winners of the first Nursery race of the season were foaled between just twenty-five days (23rd March—16th April) in their respective years, and many people believe that knowledge of foaling dates is an important weapon for the punter against the bookmaker in all two-year-old races.

Last year's one hundred and twenty-nine Nursery events were dominated by horses foaled between February and March.

89.1% of all Nursery winners were born in February, March and April last year, and I have listed the races in monthly groups, which should make the comparisons easier to follow.

You might note that juveniles foaled in May have a much better record towards the end of the season, when they have grown in strength as a result of the passing months.

Nursery races won in July 2004:

By January foaled winners: Nil
February: 9 (37.5%)
March: 10 (41.7%)
April: 5 (20.8%)
May: Nil

Races won in August:
January foals: 2 (6.1%)
February: 12 (36.4%)
March: 7 (21.2%)
April: 11 (33.3%)
May: 1 (3.0%)

Races won in September:
January foals: 1 (2.2%)
February: 14 (31.1%)
March: 19 (42.2%)
April: 8 (17.8%)
May: 3 (6.7%)

Races won in October/November:
January foals: Nil
February: 2 (7.4%)
March: 11 (40.8%)
April: 7 (25.9%)
May: 7 (25.9%)

The October and November results are particularly interesting as April/May foals won over fifty per cent of the races, which were generally won by outsiders; hence this is a route you could arguably take to win more than your fair share of profitable gains late doors in the season.

To outline the point, consider the average prices for winners during the course of the Nursery season:

Nursery races won in July: 4/1
August: 4/1
September: 9/2
October/November: 8/1

Cynics will argue that fields are bigger towards the close of the season, which is a fair point to make. My argument suggests that you need all the help you can obtain when searching for decent priced winners, and these are some of the best stats you will find.

Breeding plays an important part in the Nursery race sector, so you should be looking at speedsters in the main, certainly in the early part of the season, when most two-year-old races are contested over five and six furlongs.

It's worth noting that ex-sprinters such as Mind Games and Sri Pekan were responsible for early winners last year, though really genuine types like Mister Baileys and Danehill Dancer will produce stock to win any race!

COURSE BY COURSE INFORMATION

Ascot (2 nursery events): |
Although there will be no racing at the Berkshire venue for a while, some readers will retain this publication for years to come (hopefully) and draw reference for future use.

Three of the seven horses that carried weights of 9–1 or more finished in the frame, which compares favourably with horses down the handicap which could only record figures of 3/14.

The three shortest priced runners all rewarded toteplacepot supporters, though the strongest in the market (a 15/8 chance) was beaten into second place by a 10/1 shot.

Eighteen horses started at odds of 9/2 or more, and only three representatives managed to sneak into the frame, albeit a 40/1 chance trained by Roger Ingram was amongst them.

David Loder (8/1), John Dunlop (12/1) and Andrew Balding (12/1) were among the trainers who saddled unplaced runners.

The lesson to learn, perhaps, is that well supported runners will perform better than those which represent top trainers, who are attempting to find opportunities for what are probably ordinary horses.

Draw and full result details:

July 10: 6–3–1 (9 ran) 6 furlongs—Good (soft in places)

M. Bell	9–1	L. Dettori	3/1 fav
M. Johnston	9–7	J. Fanning	10/3
R. Hannon	9–1	R. Hughes	11/2

Sep 26: 3–9–12 (12) 7 furlongs—Good-to-firm

A. Jarvis	8–6	K. McEvoy	10/1
N. Callaghan	8–3	A. Mullen	15/8 fav
R. Ingram	8–9	S. Drowne	40/1

Ayr (5 nursery events):

Three of the six top weighted horses reached the frame which included two winners at 9/2 and 100/30. The market leaders achieved the same stats as far as placed horses were concerned, though none of the favourites actually won their respective events.

The two shortest priced runners (9/4 & 3/1) both reached the frame, as did 11/20 of the horses that started at odds of 8/1 or less. The other four places were made up from thirty-five runners priced at 10/1 or more. Only one horse was placed from eighteen raiders when starting at 20/1 or more.

Four of the five winners came from the front five in the market.

Six of the fourteen runners that carried weights of nine stones or more made the frame, with horses that carried 8–13 or less faring less well, recording stats of 5/30. Horses weighted between 7–12 and 8–1 (inclusive) achieved figures of 4/11 as far as toteplacepot material is concerned however.

Mark Johnston saddled three horses, producing a winner at 9/2 and a placed horse at 4/1. His only unplaced representative started at 12/1. Michael Bell also claimed two toteplacepot victories (without saddling a winner) via four raiders during the course of the season.

Draw and full result details:

July 19: 6–4–1 (8 ran) 6 furlongs—Good-to-firm

P.D. Evans	8–8	R. Winston	8/1
M. Bell	9–7	K. Fallon	7/2 jt fav
M. Johnston	9–3	J. Fanning	4/1

(unplaced jt fav—T. Barron—8–5—K. Darley—7/2)

Sep 17: 6–8–5 (10) 6 furlongs—Soft

B. Hills	8–5	A. Culhane	7/2
K. Ryan	8–12	N. Callan	10/1
T. Barron	8–1	P. Fessey	8/1

(unplaced fav—M. Johnston—9–6—J. Fanning—10/3)

Sep 18: 10–1–6 (11) 1 mile—Soft (heavy in places)

Sir M. Prescott	9–8	S. Sanders	10/3
M. Channon	8–11	A. Culhane	3/1 fav
G. Butler	8–12	P. Hanagan	10/3

Oct 11: 7–11–4 (14) 6 furlongs—Soft (good-to-soft in places)

T. Easterby	7–12	P. Quinn	33/1
J.J. Quinn	9–1	R. Winston	9/4 fav
M.W. Easterby	8–1	Dale Gibson	16/1

Oct 12: 4–5–6 (12) 1 mile—Good-to-soft (soft in places)

M. Johnston	9–7	K. Darley	9/2
M. Tompkins	9–0	N. Callan	10/1
M. Bell	7–12	Hayley Turner	5/1

(unplaced fav—Jedd O'Keefe—8–12—P. Hanagan—4/1)

Bath (3 nursery events): 1

Four of the five horses that started at 9/2 or less gained toteplacepot positions, though just one of the quintet actually won its respective event as a 9/2 joint favourite.

Two of the three horses that started at 12/1 ran well, gaining a gold and a silver medal in the process, though only four of the other thirty-five runners which started at 5/1 or more managed to trouble the judge.

The three winners all carried weights between 8–4 and 8–13, though four of the seven runners that were burdened with 9–3 or more reached the frame. The winner carrying 8–4, however, was the only horse from seventeen runners that carried 8–6 or less to get involved in the finish.

Rod Millman was the trainer to follow with three of his four runners reaching the frame, including a 9/2 winner.

Draw and full result details:

Sep 6: 3–11–1 (12 ran) 1 mile—Firm

P. Phelan	8–7	J. Egan	20/1
P. Cole	8–9	N. De Souza	12/1
R. Hannon	9–7	R.L. Moore	10/3 fav

Sep 13: 9–10–11 (12) 5 and a half furlongs—Good

B. Millman	8–4	A. Daly	9/2 jt fav
J.S. Moore	9–4	N. Mackay	9/2 jt fav
B. Meehan	8–7	K. Fallon	9/1

Oct 10: 13–16–18—12 (19) 5 furlongs—Good-to-soft (good in places)

R. Hollinshead	8–13	D. Sweeney	12/1
B. Millman	9–2	G. Baker	3/1 fav
B. Millman	9–3	S. Drowne	14/1
S. Kirk	9–5	J. Egan	7/1

Beverley (2 nursery events):

The two shortest priced runners both finished in the frame, with the more fancied 11/4 chance actually winning his event. Nine horses started at odds of 9/1 or less, four of which rewarded toteplacepot supporters.

Just three of the seventeen runners starting at 10/1 or more troubled the judge, though a 20/1 winner was among the mix. Horses burdened with 9–5 or more failed to run well, despite the fact that many supporters of these races tend to look at the top of the weights for inspiration.

Four of the five horses that carried weights between 8–13

and 9–4 (inclusive) reached the frame, which included the two winners at 20/1 and 11/4 (favourite).

Just two of the aggregate of fifteen runners lower down the two handicaps (8–12 or less) made the frame.

Draw and full result details:

Aug 29: 4–3–1 (10 ran) 5 furlongs—Good-to-soft

M. Johnston	9–2	R. Hills	11/4 fav
J.J. Quinn	8–13	R. Winston	4/1
B. McMahon	8–2	G. Gibbons	22/1

Sep 15: 15–7–11–10 (16) 7 and a half furlongs—Good-to-firm (firm in places)

Ron Thompson	9–4	K. McEvoy	20/1
J. Hetherton	8–13	R. Winston	7/1
A. Dickman	8–8	P. Hanagan	9/1
R. Whitaker	9–6	Dean McKeown	12/1

(unplaced fav—Mrs J. Ramsden—9–7—A. Culhane—9/2)

Brighton (2 nursery events):

Seven runners started at 8/1 or less at Brighton, with five of them finishing in the frame. The three shortest priced runners all claimed toteplacepot positions, though just the 4/5 chance rewarded win only punters. Only one of the eleven runners offered at higher odds troubled the judge.

The three top weighted horses (9–6 & 9–7) finished in the money, though, by comparison, just three of fifteen horses managed the same fate when carrying 9–4 or less.

Both of Neville Callaghan's raiders (9/2 & 20/1) finished down the field.

Draw and full result details:

July 19: 4–9–3 (9 ran) 7 furlongs—Good-to-firm

M. Bell	8–4	J. Quinn	8/1
M. Channon	9–7	T. Durcan	6/1
T. Mills	9–6	L. Dettori	2/1 fav

Sep 23: 6–2–1 (9) 6 furlongs—Firm (Good-to-firm in places)

J. Osborne	9–7	L. Dettori	4/5 fav
D. Simcock	8–5	C. Catlin	4/1
S. Kirk	8–7	J. Egan	16/1

Carlisle (1 nursery event):

Not too much to report with just the one event on the calendar.

Twelve runners started at odds of 14/1 or more, without any of them troubling the judge. The four placed runners came from the front seven horses in the betting.

Draw and full result details:

Sep 2: 1–9–3–6 (19 ran) 6 furlongs—Good (good in places)

J. Best	9–0	N. Pollard	12/1
B. Mactaggart	9–6	R. Ffrench	12/1
Mrs J.Ramsden	8–10	A. Beech	5/1 fav
M. Bell	8–6	R. Mullen	8/1

Unplaced runners (listed in finishing order) were saddled from the following stables:

P. Haslam (25/1)—R.P. Elliott (20/1)—D. Nicholls (25/1)—R. Fahey (6/1) R. Fisher (12/1)—M.W. Easterby (10/1)—N. Tinkler (40/1)—T.D. Easterby (14/1) M. Hammond (16/1)—M.W. Easterby (25/1)—J. Norton (20/1)—J. Hetherton (25/1)—T.D. Barron (20/1)—W. Brisbourne (14/1)—A. Berry (20/1).

Catterick (7 nursery events): ∿

It's worth noting that six of the seven winners at Catterick carried a minimum weight of 8–12, whilst nine of the sixteen placed horses also came via this sector of the respective handicaps.

Ninety-four horses contested the seven events, with seventeen of the twenty-three toteplacepot positions claimed by runners that started in single figure stalls. Bearing in mind that an average of more than thirteen horses contested each race, winning stall positions of 7–4–7–3–6–2–2 makes for interesting reading.

Draw and full result details:

July 21: 7–1–2 (12 ran) 7 furlongs—Good-to-firm

M. Johnston	9–6	J. Fanning	7/4 fav
P. Haslam	7–6	D. Fentiman	16/1
T. Barron	8–7	P. Makin	9/2

Aug 13: 4–2–7 (9) 6 furlongs—Soft (heavy in places)

M. Tompkins	9–4	N. Mackay	3/1
R. Fahey	8–8	P. Hanagan	11/4
J. Bethell	8–12	A. Culhane	8/1

(unplaced fav—M. Johnston—9–5—R. Ffrench—5/2)

Sep 7: 7–1–2 (14) 5 furlongs—Good-to-firm (firm in places)

M. Brittain	8–12	T. Williams	12/1
M.W. Easterby	8–1	Dale Gibson	10/1
A. Berry	9–7	F. Norton	3/1 fav

Sep 18: 3–5–1–8 (18) 7 furlongs—Firm (good-to-firm in places)

M. Johnston	9–7	R. Ffrench	9/2 fav
B. Smart	9–5	D. McGaffin	5/1
T. Easterby	8–5	J. Bramhill	7/1
Mrs J.Ramsden	9–2	L. Goncalves	14/1

Oct 5: 6–9–15–12 (17) 7 furlongs—Good (good-to-firm in places)

B. Mactaggart	9–0	Dale Gibson	10/1
N. Callaghan	9–0	K. Fallon	4/1 fav
M. Bell	8–8	J. Mackay	20/1
K. Burke	9–6	Darren Williams	25/1

Oct 16: 2–15–14 (14) 7 furlongs—Good-to-soft

P.D. Evans	8–3	T. Queally	14/1
T. Easterby	8–11	D. Allan	9/1
T. Barron	9–0	N. Callan	50/1

(unplaced far—M. Johnston—9–7—S. Chin—7/2)

Nov 2: 2–9–7 (10) 6 furlongs—Soft (heavy in places)

T. Easterby	9–3	P. Quinn	3/1
S. Kirk	8–12	J. Egan	11/2
M. Tompkins	9–2	P. Robinson	11/1

(unplaced fav—Howard Johnson—9–3—P. Mulrennan—2/1)

Chepstow (4 nursery events):

Three of the four winners at Chepstow were market leaders, whilst second favourites also claimed toteplacepot positions in seventy-five per cent of the contests.

Only two horses carried more than nine stones to good effect, with the other eight place positions being claimed by horses on or below that mark.

Draw and full result details:

Aug 5: 5–1–7 (8 ran) 6 furlongs—Good-to-firm

W. Kittow	8–5	D. Kinsella	4/1
R. Hannon	9–5	D. Holland	8/11 fav
J. Bradley	8–10	S. Whitworth	33/1

Aug 12: 3–1 (6) 6 furlongs—Good-to-soft

J. Osborne	9–7	D. Holland	15/8 fav
R. Hannon	8–9	R.L. Moore	3/1

Aug 30: 5–1 (6) 5 furlongs—Soft

A. Carroll	9–0	D. Holland	11/4 fav
W. Turner	8–1	C. Haddon	9/1

Sep 20: 6–11–10 (9) 5 furlongs—Heavy

W. Muir	8–8	S. Sanders	2/1 fav
A. Balding	8–9	L. Keniry	5/2
P.D. Evans	9–0	Joanna Badger	16/1

Chester (5 nursery events):

Richard Fahey was very much the trainer to follow at Chester, having saddled two winners at 8/1 and 11/4, with a placed horse (9/4) thrown in for good measure.

Horses carrying weights of 8-9 or more claimed twelve of the fourteen toteplacepot positions that were up for grabs, including four of the five winners.

The effect of the draw is always a talking point when discussing races at this venue, but outside of a 1-3-2 finish in a ten-runner event in August, horses drawn *high* faired well in Nursery races in the main.

Draw and full result details:

July 9: 2–8–1 (8 ran) 5 furlongs—Good

N. Littmoden	8–12	I. Mongan	7/2 fav
P.D. Evans	8–9	E. Ahern	11/1
I. Wood	8–11	R. Hughes	9/2

Aug 1: 10–7–9 (9) 6 furlongs—Good-to-firm

R. Fahey	9–7	P. Hanagan	8/1
P.D. Evans	8–9	F. Ferris	8/1
A. Bailey	8–6	D. Allan	16/1
(unplaced fav—K. Ryan—8–13—N. Callan—10/3)			

Aug 19: 1–3–2 (10) 5 furlongs—Good (good-to-soft in places)

K. Ryan	8–2	A. Mullen	Evs fav
R. Fahey	8–11	P. Hanagan	9/4
T. Easterby	8–10	D. Allan	14/1

Aug 20: 4–9–7 (9) 7 furlongs—Soft

R. Fahey	9–1	T. Hamilton	11/4 fav
W. Jarvis	9–7	K. Fallon	9/2
M. Bell	8–13	M. Fenton	9/1

Sep 11: 7–1 (7) 7 furlongs—Good

Sir M. Prescott	9–3	M. Hills	11/4
M. Tompkins	8–9	N. Callan	6/1
(unplaced fav—M. Channon—9–7—C. Catlin—9/4)			

Doncaster (7 nursery events): ◯

There were more Nursery runners at Doncaster (108) than at any other venue and horses that were well supported (6/1 or less) did well in the main. Ten of the twenty three runners reached the frame, though the shortest priced favourite at 7/4 was out of the money. Three of the eleven horses that were sent off between 11/4 and 5/1 won, returning a level stake profit of £4.75.

Conversely, only two of the thirty two runners that were sent off at 22/1 or more troubled the judge and none at all from the thirteen representatives at 40/1+.

Eleven horses carried weights of 9–6 or more on Town Moor in Nursery races in 2004, and not one of them finished in the frame! Three horses down at the other end of the weights managed to claim a toteplacepot position, though it took forty two representatives to achieve that ratio via horses that carried 8–7 or less.

It was the middle ground area of the weights that proved successful at Doncaster, returning figures of 21/55 via burdens between 8–8 and 9–5 (inclusive). All seven winners carried weights between 8–6 and 9–4.

Draw and full result details:

July 22: 4–1–6 (8 ran) 5 furlongs—Good-to-firm

M. Channon	9–4	S. Hitchcott	11/4
P.D. Evans	9–2	F. Ferris	4/1
T. Easterby	8–12	D. Allan	20/1

(Unplaced fav—J.Osborne—9–12—D. Holland—7/4)

Sep 8: 22–15–21–13 (21) 6 and a half furlongs—Good (good-to-firm in places)

S'd B Suroor	8–13	L. Dettori	5/1
B. Meehan	8–5	C. Catlin	33/1
M. Channon	8–13	T. Durcan	20/1
M. Channon	8–8	A. Culhane	12/1

(unplaced fav—T. Barron—9–2—N. Mackay—9/2)

Sep 9: 9–1–12–3 (17) 1 mile—Good-to-firm

J. Osborne	8–6	S. Drowne	20/1
M. Tompkins	8–2	P. Robinson	8/1
B. Smart	8–13	F. Lynch	33/1
J. Noseda	9–0	E. Ahern	6/1 jt fav

(unplaced jt fav—B. Meehan—8–13—L. Dettori)

Sep 11: 11–4–10 (14) 7 furlongs—Firm (good-to-firm in places)

J. Glover	8–12	F. Norton	20/1
Mrs J. Ramsden	9–1	J. Fortune	8/1
N. Littmoden	8–10	K. Fallon	4/1 fav

Oct 22: 3–10–12–14 (14) 1 mile—Soft (heavy in places)

J. Dunlop	8–8	I. Mongan	14/1
J. Dunlop	8–13	R. Hills	16/1
M. Johnston	9–3	K. Darley	10/1

(unplaced jt favs—R. Hannon—9–6—R. Hughes & S'd B Suroor—9–3—L. Dettori 9/2)

Oct 23: 1–3–12 (14) 7 furlongs—Soft (heavy in places)

M. Johnston	9–2	R. Ffrench	5/1
R. Hannon	9–1	R.L. Moore	11/1
B. Mactaggart	8–9	Dale Gibson	14/1

(unplaced fav—J. Osborne—9–0—S. Sanders—4/1)

Nov 6: 5–9–7–18 (20) 7 furlongs—Soft (good-to-soft in places)

R. Fahey	8–11	P. Hanagan	16/1
D. H'n Jones	9–1	L. Dettori	5/1 fav
J.J. Quinn	9–3	R. Winston	8/1
T. Easterby	9–5	D. Allan	14/1

Epsom (2 nursery events):

The shortest priced favourite (3/1) rewarded toteplacepot and win punters alike at Epsom from the two Nursery races last season. The three shortest priced horses after that success all failed to trouble the judge, however, whilst three of the five runners starting between 7/1 and 8/1 reached the frame (including one winner—level stake profit of 4 points).

Only two of the sixteen outsiders (10/1 & 20/1) rewarded

each-way support from horses returned between 9/1 and 33/1.

Mick Quinn saddled two Nursery horses that finished outside the money at Epsom during the season, and the ex-footballer might not be so keen to make the journey to Tattenham Corner from his new base in Newmarket this term!

Ed Dunlop suffered the same fate from as many runners, whilst other top trainers to saddle fancied horses without any luck were Richard Hannon (4/1 fav), David Loder (6/1) and Jamie Osborne (9/1)

Two of the three top weighted horses (9–7) claimed tote-placepot positions, though light weighted runners duplicated the feat, with two of the four runners carrying 8–5 or less finishing in the money at rewarding odds (20/1 & 7/1).

Draw and full result details:

Sep 9: 2–11–5 (14 ran) 6 furlongs—Good-to-firm (good in places)

M. Channon	9–7	J. Quinn	3/1 fav
D. Simcock	8–5	M. Fenton	20/1
Miss E. Lavelle	9–2	S. Kelly	10/1

Oct 2: 1–5–4 (11) 5 furlongs—Good

P. Makin	9–0	D. Sweeney	8/1
B. Millman	7–11	D. Fox	7/1
R. Bastiman	9–7	R. French	8/1

(unplaced fav—R. Hannon—8–11—R.L. Moore—4/1)

Folkestone (1 nursery event):

Top weighted horses claimed the two places that rewarded toteplacepot punters in the one Nursery race contested at Folkestone last term.

Trainers of the unplaced runners:

R. Hannon (7/2)—I. Wood (3/1)—M. Quinlan (14/1)—P. Phelan (25/1)

Draw and full result details:

Aug 5: 3–2 (6 ran) 7 furlongs—Good-to-firm (firm in places)

| V. Smith | 9–0 | T. Durcan | 5/1 |
| M. Tompkins | 9–7 | L. Dettori | 6/4 fav |

Goodwood (6 nursery events):

The Sussex venue produces some of the more feisty Nursery contests of the season, with plenty of activity in the market to set the pulses racing before flagfall. Five of the six shortest priced runners finished in the frame, though it was one of the two 7/4 chances that let the side down from achieving a clean sweep for market leaders. On the negative side, it's worth noting that only one of these short priced raiders (3/1) actually won the respective event.

All fourteen outsiders sent off at 25/1 or more were unsighted, though fourteen of the thirty nine horses ranging between 5/1 and 20/1 in the betting were successful from an each-way perspective, including five winners!

Six of the ten horses carrying weights of 9–5 or more rewarded support from a toteplacepot perspective, as did three of the five runners down at the other end of the handicap between 7–12 and 8–1.

Five of the nine runners carrying weights between 8–8 and 8–10 (inclusive) attracted the eye of the judge which included two winners at 8/1 and 5/1. Both horses were saddled by Richard Hannon and ridden by Ryan Moore.

The downhill speedtrack held no fears for Lisa Jones, as the underrated pilot steered home a 20/1 winner for Gary Moore.

Draw and full result details:

July 31: 7–3–2 (9 ran) 6 furlongs—Good-to-firm

R. Hannon	8–8	R.L. Moore	13/2
M. Channon	8–10	S. Hitchcott	10/3 fav
R. Hannon	8–1	R. Smith	14/1

July 31: 7–4–8 (9) 7 furlongs—Good-to-firm

G.L. Moore	8–3	Lisa Jones	20/1
I. Wood	8–13	K. Fallon	7/1
B. Millman	8–5	T. Durcan	8/1

(unplaced fav—M. Channon—9–4—S. Hitchcott—7/4)

Aug 27: 5–1 (6) 5 furlongs—Soft (heavy in places)

| R. Hannon | 8–8 | R.L. Moore | 5/1 |
| W. Muir | 7–12 | P. Hanagan | 6/1 |

(Unplaced fav—M.F. Harris—9–3—D. Holland—7/2)

Sep 12: 4–7–9 (8) 6 furlongs—Good-to-firm

G. Butler	9–7	L. Dettori	3/1
J. Osborne	8–13	S. Drowne	7/4 fav
W. Muir	7–12	Lisa Jones	10/1

Sep 30: 12–18–6–4 (17) 1 mile—Good (good-to-firm in places)

D. Elsworth	9–5	T. Quinn	14/1
M. Johnston	9–6	R. Ffrench	15/2
Sir M. Prescott	9–10	S. Sanders	3/1 fav
W. Kittow	8–8	D. Kinsella	20/1

Oct 10: 5–7–6–13 (16) 7 furlongs—Good-to-soft

W. Muir	8–11	R. Miles	16/1
P. Ch'l-Hyam	9–7	J. Quinn	9/4 fav
N. Littmoden	8–10	J. Guillambert	20/1
J. Dunlop	9–6	T. Quinn	9/1

Hamilton (3 nursery events):

The three winners came from the eight shortest priced Nursery runners during the season at Hamilton.

The split between fancied runners and outsiders is there for all to see at the Scottish venue, as six of the ten horses starting at odds of 6/1 or less finished in the money, compared to a success rate of 1/16 for runners sent off at 7/1 or more.

Top weighted horses were also well supported in the market. Outside of a disappointing 3/1 chance carrying 9–7, six of the next ten weights were successfully represented, compared to a ratio of just 1/14 for runners carrying 8–9 or less.

Paul Blockley saddled a 9/2 winning favourite alongside placed horses at 6/1 and 5/1 from just the three runners during the season.

Karl Burke saddled the 3/1 raider already mentioned along with an unplaced outsider, whilst negative comments can also be applied to Alan Berry, albeit that the trainer only sent two outsiders to post.

Draw and full result details:

July 16: 2–3 (6 ran) 6 furlongs—Good-to-firm

R. Fisher	8–11	R. Winston	7/2
M. Johnston	9–6	J. Fanning	5/2 fav

July 31: 5–4 (6) 6 furlongs—Good-to-firm (firm in places)

R. Bastiman	7–12	P. Hanagan	11/2
P. Blockley	9–2	Dean McKeown	6/1

(unplaced fav—A. Dickman—9–2—P. Makin—Evs)

Sep 19: 15–5–11 (14) 6 furlongs—Soft (Good-to-soft in places)

P. Blockley	9–6	M. Fenton	9/2 fav
K. Ryan	8–11	R. Winston	16/1
P. Blockley	8–12	G. Gibbons	5/1

Haydock (5 nursery events):

Three of the five events at Haydock were contested on soft/heavy ground, which makes life extremely difficult for young racehorses. It was hardly surprising, in the circumstances, that just one horse of the seven burdened with weights of 9–6 or more made it into the frame.

Conditions would have helped horses lower down the weights, and it's worth noting that three runners carried 8–3 during the season at Haydock, and they all won at 25/1—12/1—9/2 (fav)! Twelve other runners carried weights of 8–2 or less however, and all finished out of the frame. Draw your own conclusions!

The shortest priced (Kevin Ryan trained) favourite finished out of the money at 13/8, though five other runners priced at 9/2 or less troubled the judge (including three winners) from ten representatives.

All eleven outsiders sent off at 33/1 or more finished out of the frame.

Alan Berry enjoyed a fine Nursery season at Haydock. Alan claimed the media spotlight for the wrong reasons during 2004, though his efforts at Haydock would have pleased the trainer and his team. Sending just four runners to post, Alan saddled two winners at 12/1 and 3/1, whilst an 11/1 chance claimed the runner up spot on another occasion. A 12/1 raider was the only unplaced representative of the quartet.

Richard Hannon sent just the one Nursery raider up to Haydock during the year, and Spaced obliged at 20/1, in the hands of Richard Hughes.

Draw and full result details:

July 17: 5–6–2 (9 ran) 5 furlongs—Soft

A Berry	8–3	F. Norton	12/1
P.D. Evans	8–6	K. Fallon	4/1 co fav
James Moffatt	8–7	R. Winston	9/1

(unplaced co favs—M. Quinlan—9–7—P. McCabe & B. Smart—9–7—F. Lynch)

Aug 6: 3–11–4 (12) 5 furlongs—Good

M.W. Easterby	8–3	R. Ffrench	25/1
A. Berry	8–13	F. Norton	11/1
A. Balding	8–11	S. Sanders	8/1

(unplaced fav—K. Ryan—9–7—N. Callan—13/8)

Aug 12: 3–7 (6) 6 furlongs—Heavy

| A. Berry | 9–0 | F. Norton | 3/1 |
| K. Ryan | 9–4 | N. Callan | 2/1 fav |

Sep 4: 6–1–4 (11) 1 mile—Good

R. Hannon	9–2	R. Hughes	20/1
M. Channon	9–2	T. Durcan	7/2
A. Jarvis	9–0	K. McEvoy	11/1

(unplaced fav—G. Butler—9–7—J. Murtagh—5/2)

Sep 24: 4–15–3 (15) 6 furlongs—Heavy (soft in places)

R. Fahey	8–3	P. Hanagan	9/2 fav
T. Easterby	9–7	D. Allan	16/1
M. Channon	9–4	A. Culhane	10/1

Kempton (2 nursery events):

Although there will be no racing at Sunbury for a while, some readers will retain this publication for years to come and draw reference for future use.

Richard Hannon was weaving his magic spell over the opposition again at Kempton in 2004, scoring with his lone raider at 14/1! David Evans also faired well at the Sunbury circuit, saddling a 5/1 winner alongside a runner-up, though the trainer might have expected a better effort from a 6/5 chance.

Rod Millman suffered two reversals at Kempton (6/1 & 9/1), whilst top handlers such as David Loder, Mick Channon, Michael Bell and Jamie Osborne all left Kempton empty handed.

Aside from the 6/5 favourite reaching the frame, other fancied horses (10/1 or less) disappointed punters by only recording two other placed efforts from eleven representatives. Outsiders faired well by comparison, as two of the five runners priced at 14/1 or more rewarded each-way support.

The old adage of back the top weights in Nursery races was shot down in flames again, as the two horses at the top of the handicaps could summon just a placed effort at 6/5 between them.

Draw and full result details:

July 28: 5–6–3 (10) 6 furlongs—Good-to-firm

P. D. Evans	9–1	S. Donohoe	5/1
D. Coakley	8–9	E. Ahern	20/1
P. McEntee	8–4	F. Ferris	7/1

Unplaced jt favs—J. Spearing—9–7—L. Dettori—9/2 & D. Haydn Jones—9–2—Paul Eddery)

Aug 4: 4–3 (7 ran) 6 furlongs—Good-to-firm (good in places)

R. Hannon	8–5	R. Smith	14/1
P. D. Evans	9–3	S. Donohoe	6/5 fav

Leicester (4 nursery events):   ⟳

Horses from the middle of the handicap upwards performed well in the main, with eight of the twenty five runners weighted with 8–10 or more claiming toteplacepot positions, compared to figures of 4/29 from those burdened with 8–9 or less.

Three of the four winners carried weights of either 9–6 or 9–7 from just four representatives, though a one pound level stake only amounted to ten pounds profit.

Three of the four shortest priced runners (9/2 or less) reached the frame (including two winners) as did three of the five horses returned at either 11/1 or 12/1. Just three of the outsiders priced at 14/1 or more claimed toteplacepot positions from thirty representatives.

Draw and full result details:

July 15: 16–12–15 (14 ran) 6 furlongs—Good-to-firm (good in places)

B. Millman	7–13	F. Norton	16/1
S. Kirk	8–10	K. McEvoy	8/1
W. Turner	8–0	C. Haddon	14/1

(unplaced co favs—D. Loder—8–8—T. Queally—5/1——J. O'Reilly—9–7—D. Allen——B. McMahon—8–12—W. Supple)

July 21: 6–1 (7) 5 furlongs—Good-to-firm (good in places)

| R. Charlton | 9–7 | D. Sweeney | Evs fav |
| D. Nicholls | 8–5 | A. Nicholls | 6/1 |

Sep 7: 8–15–13–10 (20) 7 furlongs—Good-to-firm (good in places)

R. J-Houghton	9–6	L. Dettori	9/2 jt fav
P. Blockley	8–10	I. Mongan	12/1
Mrs J.Ramsden	9–4	K. Fallon	9/2 jt fav
W. Musson	9–0	R. Hughes	11/1

Sep 20: 8–10–4 (13) 6 furlongs—Good-to-soft

B. Meehan	9–6	R. Winston	13/2
Mrs H.Sweet'g	8–5	P. Doe	25/1
J. Eustace	8–12	J. Tate	12/1

(unplaced fav—E. Dunlop—8–6—A. Culhane—9/2)

Lingfield (5 nursery events): 2 FAV

The two shortest priced horses both reached the frame, though four runners ranging between 9/4 and 4/1 finished unplaced in their respective contests.

Five of the eight horses returned at 6/1 and 7/1 finished in the money, including three winners.

Only two horses that carried 9–3 or more troubled the judge from twenty-two representatives. Six of the eight runners that carried either 8–7 or 8–8 finished in the frame by comparison, including two winners.

All ten horses that carried weights of 8–6 or less finished out of the money.

Draw and full result details:

July 7: 6–3 (6 ran) 6 furlongs—Good-to-firm (firm in places)

| J. Osborne | 8–8 | S. Kelly | 7/1 |
| D. Loder | 9–2 | N. Pollard | 7/1 |

(unplaced fav—E. Dunlop—9–0—R. Mullen—9/4)

July 17: 2–3–12 (12) 5 furlongs—Good

J. Osborne	8–13	E. Ahern	6/1
Mrs C. Dunnett	8–11	Hayley Turner	9/1
E. Dunlop	9–0	L. Dettori	2/1 fav

Sep 7: 17–11–8–7 (20) 7 furlongs—Good-to-firm

Sir M. Stoute	9–2	N. Mackay	7/1 fav
N. Littmoden	9–2	J. Guillambert	12/1
B. Millman	8–8	S. Drowne	25/1
N. Callaghan	9–0	O. Urbina	10/1

Sep 22: 7–1–4–17 (10) 7 furlongs—Good-to-firm

N. Callaghan	9–6	O. Urbina	4/5 fav
B. Meehan	9–2	J. McDonald	16/1
P. Harris	8–8	I. Mongan	40/1
E. Dunlop	9–5	S. Drowne	16/1

Oct 1: 9–14–15–10 (17) 7 furlongs—Good-to-firm

B. Millman	8–8	P. Doe	10/1
Mrs H. Sweet'g	8–12	G. Baker	6/1 jt fav
J. Pearce	8–7	J. Quinn	25/1
W. Muir	8–8	D. Kinsella	33/1

(unplaced jt fav—R. Hannon—8–4—R. Thomas)

Musselburgh (5 nursery events): 2

Watch for any horse that Sir Mark Prescott saddles in this sector, as Succession won two races for the trainer in as many starts at Musselburgh, and this was Mark's only raider all year!

Although a top weight of 9–11 could not stop a Mark Johnston good thing from scoring at odds of 8/15, only one other horse carried nine stone or more to good effect from fourteen representatives.

Horses further down the handicap ran well generally, with seven of the eighteen runners carrying 8–5 or less finishing in the frame, including those at 33/1, 25/1, 16/1 and 12/1.

Six of the nine horses at the other end of the betting spectrum (priced at 5/1 or less) claimed toteplacepot positions, though just two of them actually won their respective races at 9/2 and 8/15.

Draw and full result details:

July 29: 1–3 (6 ran) 7 furlongs—Good-to-firm (firm in places)

| M. Johnston | 9–11 | S. Chin | 8/15 fav |
| T. D. Barron | 8–5 | P. Makin | 8/1 |

Aug 26: 7–4–12 (12) 5 furlongs—Good-to-firm (good in places)

J. S. Moore	8–2	N. Mackay	9/2
T. Easterby	8–4	D. Allan	7/2
M. Dods	7–12	P. Fessey	25/1

(unplaced fav—R. Bastiman—9–1—R. Ffrench—11/4)

Sep 11: 8–9–6 (14) 1 mile—Good (good-to-firm in places)

Sir M. Prescott	8–11	J. Mackay	7/1
P. Haslam	8–11	G. Faulkner	16/1
C. Fairhurst	7–13	Leanne Kershaw	33/1

(unplaced fav—T. D. Barron—9–0—P. Makin—4/1)

Sep 13: 12–8–3 (13) 5 furlongs—Good-to-firm (good in places)

A. Berry	7–13	F. Norton	12/1
R. Bastiman	8–3	A. Mullen	16/1
J. Osborne	8–11	S. Kelly	5/1 jt fav

(unplaced jt fav—N. Littmoden—9–2—I. Mongan)

Sep 26: 5–4–3 (8) 1 mile—Good-to-firm (good in places)

Sir M. Prescott	8–12	D. Holland	4/5 fav
M. Johnston	9–7	K. Darley	7/2
B. Smart	8–11	F. Lynch	7/1

Newbury (3 nursery events):

Fancied horses generally held sway at the Berkshire venue, with seven of the fifteen horses priced at 9/1 or less finishing in the money. All three winners were priced at 10/1 or less.

Eleven horses carried weights of 8–5 or less at Newbury, with just one representative able to earn a cheque for connections.

Draw and full result details:

Aug 1: 4–2–12 (11 ran) 7 furlongs—Good-to-firm

M. Magnusson	8–8	E. Ahern	10/1
B. Millman	8–9	G. Baker	8/1
D. Elsworth	8–13	S. Sanders	6/1

(unplaced fav—T. Mills—9–0—J. Fortune—9/2)

Oct 22: 8–9–11 (14) 7 furlongs—Soft (heavy in places)

P. Chapple-Hyam	8–7	Thomas Yeung	6/1
G. Butler	9–7	J. Fortune	9/2 fav
M. Johnston	8–11	J. Fanning	6/1

Oct 23: 8–14–10–9 (20) 6 furlongs—Heavy

T. Easterby	8–3	P. Quinn	9/1
S. Kirk	8–6	J. Egan	40/1
Mrs H. Sweet'g	8–6	P. Doe	12/1
P. Chapp-Hyam	9–6	D. Holland	15/2

(unplaced fav—K. Ryan—8–11—T. Quinn—13/2)

Newcastle (3 nursery events): 1 FAV

Jedd O'Keefe was the man to follow in Nursery races at Newcastle last year, as the trainer saddled a winner (16/1) and a runner up (13/2) from just the two representatives.

Only one of the four horses that carried top weight of 9–7 finished in the frame, which included an unplaced joint favourite. Horses faired no better at the other end of the handicaps, as just one of the eight runners that carried 8–2 or less finished in the money.

Five of the six runners that were priced between 9/2 and 9/1 claimed toteplacepot positions, which included two winners at 6/1 and 9/2.

Draw and full result details:

Aug 4: 9–6–3 (13 ran) 7 furlongs—Good-to-soft (good in places)

Jedd O'Keefe	7–12	J. Mackay	16/1
B. Smart	9–7	D. McGaffin	5/1
T. D. Barron	8–5	K. Darley	11/4 fav

Aug 30: 6–9–2 (9) 1 mile—Soft (heavy in places)

M. Jarvis	9–0	P. Robinson	9/2
Jedd O'Keefe	8–3	P. Hanagan	13/2
M. Bell	8–6	M. Fenton	10/1

(unplaced jt favs—M. Channon—9–0—S. Sanders—7/2 & J. Dunlop—9–7—G. Carter)

Oct 10: 2–5–7–8 (18) 6 furlongs—Good (good-to-firm in places)

K. Burke	8–12	Darren Williams	6/1 fav
P. Haslam	9–0	K. Darley	10/1
M. Channon	9–4	J. Carroll	9/1
G. M. Moore	9–3	T. Eaves	16/1

Newmarket (Rowley Mile)—6 nursery events: 3 ★☆♪

Although Richard Hannon didn't manage to saddle a winner in Nursery events on the Rowley Mile course at Newmarket last year, the popular handler was rewarded with five placed horses including those at 20/1, 16/1 (twice) and 10/1.

Brian Meehan was the other handler to note, saddling two winners at 3/1 and 2/1, which were supplemented by a placed horse at 25/1. Brian saddled just one unplaced runner in the process.

Only two of the twelve horses that carried 9–6 or 9–7 managed to finish in the money, though four of the five runners that were burdened with just 8–3 or 8–4 made the frame.

All four horses that started at 3/1 or less claimed toteplacepot positions (including three winners), though, conversely, none of the nine runners sent off at 33/1 or more were involved at the business end of their respective races.

Draw and full result details:

Sep 21: 2–8–9 (13 ran) 1 mile—Good-to-firm

B. Meehan	9–0	L. Dettori	2/1 fav
R. Hannon	8–3	R.L. Moore	5/1
M. Magnusson	8–3	E. Ahern	25/1

Sep 21: 5–6–1 (10) 6 furlongs—Good-to-firm

B. Meehan	9–4	J. Fortune	3/1 fav
R. Hannon	9–3	R.L. Moore	16/1
R. Beckett	9–7	S. Sanders	5/1

Sep 30: 4–12–11 (12) 6 furlongs—Good (good-to-soft in places)

M. Channon	9–4	A. Culhane	20/1
R. Hannon	8–8	R.L. Moore	10/1
G. Butler	9–6	J. Murtagh	9/4 fav

Oct 2: 11–13–10–15 (16) 7 furlongs—Good (good-to-soft in places)

Mrs A. Perrett	9–5	J. Murtagh	9/1
R. Hannon	8–11	K. Darley	20/1
N. Callaghan	9–3	N. Mackay	7/1
B. Meehan	9–4	S. Sanders	25/1

(unplaced fav—M. Channon—9–7—K. Fallon—6/1)

Oct 14: 10–9–6 (12) 1 mile—Soft

N. Callaghan	8–12	D. Holland	15/2
S.B. Suroor	9–4	L. Dettori	9/2
Mrs J.Ramsden	8–4	C. Catlin	20/1

(unplaced fav—Sir M. Stoute—8–10—R. Hills—7/2)

Oct 15: 9–6–10 (14) 6 furlongs—Soft

B. McMahon	9–3	G. Gibbons	15/8 fav
A. Carroll	9–0	D. Holland	12/1
R. Hannon	8–13	K. Fallon	16/1

Newmarket (July)—(7 nursery events): 4 fav

Seven different trainers saddled the winners of the respective races, though it's worth noting Mick Channon's raiders on the July course, and the popular handler rewarded supporters with three placed horses last year, which included a 50/1 chance.

Although the top weighted horse all season (9–9) failed to make the frame, eight of the sixteen horses that carried weights ranging between 9–3 and 9–8 rewarded each-way supporters, which included three winners.

Six of the seven horses that were returned at 7/2 or less

finished in the frame, including three winners.

Six of the seven winners were drawn in stalls one to six.

Draw and full result details:

July 8: 13–2–10 (13 ran) 7 furlongs—Good-to-soft

D. Loder	9–6	T. Queally	7/2 fav
M. Channon	8–11	S. Hitchcott	14/1
N. Callaghan	9–7	J. Murtagh	10/1

July 23: 4–7–6 (11) 7 furlongs—Good-to-firm

N. Callaghan	9–7	J. Murtagh	7/2 jt fav
M. Bell	7–12	J. Mackay	10/1
M. Channon	8–12	S. Hitchcott	7/2 jt fav

July 31: 5–10–4 (11) 6 furlongs—Good-to-firm

J. Eustace	8–13	S. Drowne	10/1
P. McEntee	7–9	F. Ferris	12/1
T. Easterby	8–13	W. Supple	15/2
(unplaced fav—M. Bell—9–7—J. Mackay—3/1)			

Aug 6: 5–7 (7) 7 furlongs—Good-to-firm

M. Tompkins	8–7	L. Dettori	9/4 fav
R. Hannon	9–3	Dane O'Neill	5/2

Aug 14: 1–6–12 (13) 5 furlongs—Good-to-soft

N. Littmoden	8–10	I. Mongan	33/1
R. Fahey	8–4	P. Hanagan	7/1
R. Hannon	9–7	R.L. Moore	11/2
(unplaced jt favs—T. Mills—9–7—S. Sanders—4/1 & M. Jarvis—9–2—P. Robinson)			

Aug 27: 6–11–13 (13) 1 mile—Soft

M. Bell	9–8	Hayley Turner	8/11 fav
M. Channon	8–3	J. Fanning	50/1
A. Carroll	9–1	N. Callan	20/1

Aug 28: 3–11–6–8 (16) 6 furlongs—Good-to-soft

K. Ryan	8–13	N. Callan	5/1
R. Hannon	9–3	R. Hughes	8/1
M. Johnston	9–7	K. Darley	4/1 fav
B. Hills	8–2	R. Mullen	14/1

Nottingham (4 nursery events): 3

Six of the eight horses starting at 5/1 or less claimed totepla-cepot positions (including three winners), though just four of the forty runners that were returned at 12/1 or more reached the frame.

All six horses that carried either 9–5 or 9–6 finished down the field, though it's worth noting that eight of the twenty runners burdened between 8–12 and 9–4 rewarded each-way supporters.

Draw and full result details:

Aug 16: 9–10–8 (11 ran) 5 furlongs—Good (good-to-soft in places)

K. Ryan	8–1	A. Mullen	5/4 fav
P. D. Evans	8–12	S. Drowne	14/1
B. Meehan	8–12	L. Dettori	10/1

Sep 17: 11–4–10–1 (19) 6 furlongs—Good-to-soft

P. Harris	9–11	I. Mongan	2/1 fav
E. Dunlop	9–7	E. Ahern	11/1
B. McMahon	8–13	N. Chalmers	16/1
R. Hannon	9–3	P. Dobbs	5/1

Sep 28: 12–4–14–7 (16) 10 furlongs—Good-to-firm (good in places)

N. Callaghan	9–3	K. Fallon	9/2 fav
D. Ffrench Davis	9–7	T. Quinn	11/1
P. Phelan	9–4	C. Catlin	10/1
R. Hannon	9–2	R. Hughes	11/1

Nov 4: 12–6–2–14 (16) 5 furlongs—Heavy (soft in places)

G. Butler	8–1	C. Catlin	40/1
W. Muir	8–11	Martin Dwyer	4/1
I. Wood	9–1	S. Sanders	9/2
J. Osborne	8–1	J. McDonald	66/1

(unplaced fav—P. Blockley—K. Fallon—5/2)

Pontefract (4 nursery events): ○

Three of the four shortest priced runners during the season finished in the money, though only one of them claimed the gold medal.

Forty two runners were sent off at odds of 10/1 or more, and just five of them troubled the judge, though if you extend the study to those at 20/1 or more the result is 1/26 from a toteplacepot perspective.

Draw and full result details:

July 6: 2–9–8 (9 ran) 6 furlongs—Good-to-firm

J. Bethell	8–8	T. Quinn	8/1
M. Johnston	9–7	K. Dalgleish	5/4 fav
T. D. Barron	8–0	P. Fessey	9/1

Sep 23: 8–3–10 (11) 1 mile—Firm

J. Gosden	9–7	J. Fortune	7/2
M. Channon	8–13	A. Culhane	7/2
P. Haslam	7–11	Rory Moore	25/1

(unplaced fav—Sir M. Stoute—9–2—K. Fallon—6/4)

Oct 4: 9–17–6–5 (18) 6 furlongs—Good-to-firm

S. Kirk	9–4	M. Hills	8/1
T. D. Barron	8–12	K. Darley	14/1
M. Jarvis	8–9	P. Robinson	11/2

(Unplaced fav—T. Easterby—9–7—D. Allan—9/2)

Oct 18: 16–18–2–19 (19) 1 mile—Good (good-to-soft in places)

G. M. Moore	8–13	L. Dettori	9/1
D. Arbuthnot	8–13	S. Kelly	14/1
G. Wragg	9–0	D. Holland	15/2 fav
N. Callaghan	9–0	A. Mullen	18/1

Redcar (4 nursery events):

Seven of the eleven horses that carried 9–3 or more reached the frame, though only one winner emerged from this sector, albeit the 12/1 chance helped produce a level stake profit.

Just one of the twenty-five runners that were returned at 20/1 or more troubled the judge, whilst figures of 0/15 related to horses at 33/1+.

Draw and full result details:

Aug 8: 1–8–5 (9 ran) 6 furlongs—Firm (good-to-firm in places)

R. Fahey	8–6	P. Hanagan	9/2
P. Blockley	9–5	M. Fenton	13/2
T. Easterby	9–7	D. Allen	9/2

(Unplaced fav—M. Channon—9–5—E. Ahern—4/1)

Sep 2: 17–16–20–9 (20) 7 furlongs—Good-to-firm (firm in places)

B. Smart	9–5	F. Lynch	12/1
P. Haslam	8–5	G. Faulkner	6/1
N. Littmoden	9–4	L. Fletcher	10/1
D. Loder	9–6	K. Darley	10/1

(Unplaced fav—M. Channon—8–9—A. Culhane—5/1)

Sep 13: 11–15–3 (14) 5 furlongs—Firm (good-to-firm in places)

P. D'Arcy	8–12	L. Dettori	8/1
B. Hills	9–7	R. Hughes	2/1 fav
M. W. Easterby	7–13	Dale Gibson	13/2

Nov 1: 8–18–13–20 (19) 1 mile—Soft (heavy in places)

P. Haslam	8–4	N. Pollard	9/1
John Berry	8–6	K. Darley	16/1
S. Griffiths	9–3	A. Nicholls	25/1
A. Berry	8–5	F. Norton	7/1

(Unplaced fav—R. Fahey—9–7—P. Hanagan—5/1)

Ripon (2 nursery events):

Although an 11/1 chance won the second of the two Nursery races run at Ripon last year carrying 9–3, seven other horses ran down the field when burdened between 9–0 and 9–7.

Draw and full result details:

Aug 31: 6–2–9 (10 ran) 6 furlongs—Good-to-soft (soft in places)

R. Fahey	8–3	P. Hanagan	4/1
J.J. Quinn	8–9	R. Winston	10/1
K. Ryan	8–9	N. Callan	7/1

(Unplaced fav—M. Johnston—9–2—J. Fanning—3/1)

Sep 25: 14–10–11 (15) 5 furlongs—Good-to-firm

M. Harris	9–3	A. Nicholls	11/1
M. Brittain	8–10	T. Williams	10/1
R. Hollinshead	8–6	Dale Gibson	33/1

(Unplaced fav—A. Berry—9–1—F. Norton—7/2)

Salisbury (2 nursery events):

It will surprise nobody down Salisbury way that David Elsworth won both Nursery events last term, though the starting prices of 12/1 and 6/1 took the breath away!

Only one of the ten horses that carried weights of nine stones or more made the frame, whilst it's worth noting that two of three lowest weighted horses claimed toteplacepot positions at odds of 11/1 and 10/1.

Draw and full result details:

Aug 20: 9–10–13 (12 ran) 6 furlongs—Good-to-soft

D. Elsworth	9–0	J. Fortune	6/1 co fav
D. Coakley	8–13	E. Ahern	7/1
R. Hannon	8–0	R. Smith	10/1

(Unplaced co favs—R. Hannon—8–10—R.L. Moore—D. Ffrench Davis—8–11—D. Holland & M. Channon—9–7—T. Durcan)

Sep 14: 7–5–4 (12) 1 mile—Soft (heavy in places)

D. Elsworth	8–12	J. Fortune	12/1
M. Channon	8–10	T. Dean	25/1
M. Bell	7–13	Hayley Turner	11/1

(Unplaced fav—M. Johnston—9–6—K. Fallon—13/8)

Sandown (2 nursery events):

Just one of the five horses at the top of the two handicaps managed to make the frame, whilst fancied horses also ran disappointingly.

Draw and full result details:

Aug 20: 2–3 (7 ran) 5 furlongs—Good-to-soft (soft in places)

| Sir M. Prescott | 9–7 | S. Sanders | 2/1 fav |
| Miss E. Lavelle | 9–1 | S. Drowne | 16/1 |

Aug 21: 2–6–4 (8) 7 furlongs—Soft

I. Wood	8–8	M. Fenton	20/1
M. Channon	9–3	L. Dettori	9/2
S. Kirk	8–12	J. Egan	9/1

(Unplaced fav—P. Chapple-Hyam—9–7—K. Fallon—13/8)

Thirsk (1 nursery event):

Top stables that saddled unplaced runners in the one and only Nursery race at Thirsk included Jamie Osborne (4/1), Michael Bell (5/1) and Tim Easterby (33/1).

Draw and full result details:

July 31: 1–9–8 (10 ran) 5 furlongs—Firm

R. Fahey	8–4	P. Hanagan	7/1
A. Berry	9–2	G. Hind	6/1
R. Charlton	9–4	D. Sweeney	15/8 fav

Warwick (3 nursery events):

The shortest priced runner (7/4) failed to make the frame, though five of the next six horses in the betting in the three Nursery events claimed toteplacepot positions, ranging in odds between 7/1 and 3/1.

Conversely, just one of the fifteen outsiders priced between 8/1 and 33/1 troubled the judge, albeit that a David Loder raider scored at 12/1.

1 × 3

Draw and full result details:

Aug 30: 2–4–11 (13 ran) 6 furlongs—Good-to-soft (good in places)

D. Loder	8–6	K. Darley	12/1
B. Hills	8–13	R. Hughes	3/1
E. Dunlop	8–8	E. Ahern	7/1
(Unplaced fav—J. Osborne—9–2—S. Kelly—7/4)			

Sep 6: 3–12–6 (14) 6 furlongs—Good-to-firm

P. Harris	9–0	D. Holland	9/2
J. Osborne	9–4	S. Drowne	2/1 fav
R. Hannon	9–4	Dane O'Neill	8/1

Sep 18: 1–3–4 (9) 7 furlongs—Good-to-soft

N. Callaghan	8–6	N. De Souza	4/1 jt fav
J. Osborne	9–2	S. Kelly	9/2
E. Dunlop	9–2	O. Urbina	13/2
(Unplaced jt fav—P. Makin—9–7—D. Sweeney)			

Windsor (5 nursery events):

High numbers often have the edge in sprint races at Windsor, though horses that ran from lower numbers in Nursery events

O FAV

helped to produce some great toteplacepot dividends during the course of the season.

Only four of the twelve runners that carried weights of 9–4 or more made the frame whilst similarly poor figures were returned for fancied horses at 4/1 or less. A 4/7 chance only managed second place, whilst a 6/4 favourite (trained by Neville Callaghan) finished down the field.

Draw and full result details:

Aug 9: 7–6–8 (12 ran) 6 furlongs—Good-to-soft (good in places)

K. Burke	9–2	K. Fallon	9/2
W. Brisbourne	9–3	S. Sanders	9/1
S. Kirk	8–8	J. Egan	16/1

(Unplaced fav—R. Hannon—8–13—P. Dobbs—4/1)

Aug 23: 5–4 (6) 5 furlongs—Good-to-soft

M. Bell	9–1	Hayley Turner	4/1
Sir M. Prescott	9–13	S. Sanders	4/7 fav

Sep 27: 5–6–2–8 (18) 5 furlongs—Good-to-firm

J. Osborne	9–3	E. Ahern	14/1
B. Millman	8–2	R. Mullen	25/1
P. Makin	9–1	D. Sweeney	25/1
Mrs P. Dutfield	8–12	R. Havlin	25/1

(Unplaced fav—B. Hills—9–1—R. Hughes—7/2)

Oct 4: 9–3–4 (13) 1 mile—Soft

R. Beckett	9–4	D. Holland	14/1
M. Johnston	9–3	R. Ffrench	14/1
D. Loder	9–6	S. Sanders	40/1

(Unplaced fav—N. Callaghan—9–6—L. Dettori—6/4)

Oct 11: 11–9–10 (13) 1 mile—Good (good-to-firm in places)

R. Hannon	9–6	R.L. Moore	9/2
I. Wood	8–13	P. Doe	16/1
A. King	8–13	J. Smith	14/1

(Unplaced fav—9–3—L. Keniry—4/1)

Yarmouth (6 nursery events):

James Given is a trainer to note at Yarmouth, and the popular handler saddled a 10/1 winner, alongside placed horses at 50/1 and 16/1.

The shortest priced favourite (15/8) ran unplaced, though seven of the next thirteen horses in the betting in their respective races claimed toteplacepot positions. Conversely, just three of the sixteen horses towards the top of the handicaps (9–3 or more) managed to reach the frame.

Draw and full result details: *2 × 6*

Aug 24: 8–4–5 (9 ran) 6 furlongs—Soft (good-to-soft in places)

J. Given	8–4	J. Fanning	10/1
P. Haslam	7–6	D. Fentiman	15/2
C. Dwyer	7–7	Hayley Turner	16/1

(Unplaced fav—J. Pearce—8–0—J. Quinn—10/3)

Sep 14: 7–6–14 (14) 7 furlongs—Good-to-firm

Sir M. Prescott	8–9	S. Sanders	9/4 fav
M. Channon	9–7	T. Durcan	11/2
J. Portman	9–0	N. Callan	20/1

Sep 16: 14–16–15–10 (16) 1 mile—Good (good-to-soft in places)

J. O'Shea	9–3	D. Sweeney	10/1
Miss J.Fielden	8–13	B. Reilly	16/1
J. Pearce	8–7	J. Quinn	12/1
M. Channon	7–9	T. Dean	40/1

(Unplaced fav—G. Swinbank—8–12—L. Dettori—15/8)

Sep 16: 8–7–1–9 (20) 1 mile—Good (good-to-soft in places)

N. Callaghan	9–0	L. Dettori	2/1 fav
M. Tompkins	8–6	P. Robinson	20/1
Sir M. Stoute	9–5	R. Hills	9/2
J. Given	8–11	M. Fenton	50/1

Oct 27: 2–7–3 (8) 5 furlongs—Soft (good-to-soft in places)

Mrs C. Dunnett	9–2	Hayley Turner	11/2
P. McEntee	8–6	S. Kelly	4/1
S. Kirk	9–1	J. Egan	3/1 fav

Nov 5: 13–10–17–18 (20) 1 mile—Soft (good-to-soft in places)

P. McBride	8–6	T. Queally	25/1
E. Dunlop	8–10	R. Hills	16/1
J. Dunlop	8–11	K. Darley	10/1
J. Given	8–8	P. Robinson	16/1

(Unplaced fav—N. Callaghan—9–7—D. Holland—7/1)

York (6 nursery events):

Tim Easterby is the man to follow in Nursery events at York. Although Tim saddled four unplaced runners on the Knavesmire, the popular trainer claimed two winners at 13/2 and 4/1, whilst securing placed positions at 16/1 and 6/1.

Just one of the seven horses that carried weights of 9–6 or more claimed a toteplacepot position.

All twenty-one horses that started at 20/1 or more finished unplaced.

Draw and full result details:

July 10: 6–2–8 (10 ran) 5 furlongs—Good (good-to-soft in places)

M. Bell	7–13	A. McCarthy	7/1
A. Jarvis	9–7	K. Fallon	5/1
K. Ryan	8–3	P. Fessey	11/1

(Unplaced fav—M.W. Easterby—7–10—J. McDonald—4/1)

July 24: 6–7 (7) 5 furlongs—Good (good-to-firm in places)

| T. Easterby | 9–3 | K. Darley | 4/1 |
| A. Berry | 8–8 | P. Mathers | 13/2 |

(Unplaced fav—T. Easterby—8–9—R. Winston—10/3)

Aug 17: 9–15–13 (13) 6 furlongs—Good (good-to-soft in places)

T. Easterby	8–13	K. Fallon	13/2
K. Ryan	8–7	N. Callan	10/1
P. D. Evans	8–11	S. Donohoe	16/1

(Unplaced fav—Mrs J. Ramsden—8–8—I. Mongan—3/1)

Aug 19: 2–9–4 (12) 7 furlongs—Soft

M. Bell	9–1	R. Mullen	7/2 fav
W. Kittow	7–12	A. McCarthy	16/1
R. Hannon	8–12	R.L. Moore	13/2

Sep 5: 17–16–3–11 (17) 7 furlongs—Good-to-firm (firm in places)

M. Tompkins	9–5	P. Robinson	7/1
T. Easterby	8–0	R. Ffrench	16/1
T. Easterby	9–1	D. Allan	6/1
P. Haslam	9–3	G. Faulkner	12/1

(Unplaced fav—W. Muir—S. Drowne—5/1)

Oct 8: 9–10–11 (15) 6 furlongs—Good

B. McMahon	8–3	G. Gibbons	9/1
J. Osborne	8–6	T. Queally	11/1
M.W. Easterby	8–11	Dale Gibson	11/2

(Unplaced fav—M. Johnston—9–0—K. Darley—9/2)

OFF TO A FLYER AND THE GETTING OUT STAKES!

The first and last races on any card are important, as you are searching for inspiration/confidence for the races ahead when trying to sort out the first winner of the afternoon/evening, whilst very often you are desperately seeking guidance in the Getting Out Stakes, when chasing losses late doors!

I used to be a betting shop manager many years ago, and I remember telling my old boss on one occassion that we would have had a good day as far as results had gone had it not been for the well backed favourite winning the last race. He stared at me with a puzzled look on his face asking what the last race was. I told him it was the 5.20 at Kempton (as an example), whereby he informed me that there was no such thing as the last race, the last race simply being the first race the next day, or dare I say, the first race at an evening greyhound venue that very night!

The point he was making, as we all know, is that the last race is merely a figment of our imagination, as a punter will invariably be looking up tomorrow's runners, the minute his last horse has run, win, lose or draw.

This sums up the losing punter in many ways of course, because s/he is simply looking for the next fix, irrespective of whether the event in question is a Nursery race, a three-year-old maiden or the Grand National!

Being creatures of habit, however, nothing I say will make any difference whatsoever; hence I have made a five-year study of the first and last Nursery events of the season.

The opening event at Pontefract (run on July 6th last year):

Headlines:

- Clive Brittain has saddled two horses in this event during the period and both won, at starting prices of 16/1 & 11/2.
- The last four (clear) favourites have all been beaten, including a 5/4 chance last year.
- The last two winners have followed the same path to victory. Both Prospect Court and Fragrant Star had contested two maiden races, followed by a Listed event at Ascot, and had finished unplaced each time at the Royal venue.
- None of the fourteen horses that were returned at prices of 20/1 or more has scored, though one 33/1 shot finished second in 2003.
- The last four winners were all foaled between 23rd March and the 16th April.
- All five winners had an official rating between 75 and 79 coming into this event.
- Four of the five winners carried weights ranging between eight and nine stone.

The closing event at Doncaster (run on 6th November last year):

Headlines:

- Richard Fahey has saddled three runners during the period, a winner and a placed horse which were both returned at 16/1, whilst his third (20/1) raider finished just outside the place money in fifth spot.
- Derek Haydn-Jones has saddled two runners of late, the runner-up (5/1 favourite) last year, and a 20/1 shot which was denied a toteplacepot position by a short head in 2003.
- Only one favourite has finished out of the frame in the last

five years, and that was in the most open of contests (8/1 the field) back in 2001.

- Eight of the seventeen runners that carried weights ranging between 9–1 & 9–5 claimed toteplacepot positions.
- All thirty-four horses sent off at prices of 25/1 or more finished out of the frame.
- Only five of the fifty-three horses with an official rating of 71 or less troubled the judge.
- Four of the five winners were drawn between stall numbers five and eight in average fields of twenty-one runners.

It should be noted that, at the time of writing, exact dates for this year's races had not been formulated. There is a chance that rearranged races could scupper the usual opening/closing Nursery scenarios (as with Kempton/Doncaster at the start of the season), though that situation is unlikely to occur.

NURSERY RACES AND THEIR INFLUENCE OVER TOTEPLACEPOT DIVIDENDS

The toteplacepot is arguably the most popular bet in Britain today. It has taken over twenty eight years for that scenario to occur, but few people who have a bet these days can claim they have never invested in the toteplacepot, which is not the case for a *Goliath* I'll wager!

Nursery races are handicaps pure and simple, albeit the handicapper is asked to assess two-year-olds in this sector, and we should wish the very best of luck to him/her.

These events are fiercely competitive contests in the main, which is reflected by the price of the favourites, as you will have determined by reading this publication. Such races are ideal for the toteplacepot and my study has detected that Nursery races have an incredible effect on the final dividend.

Without wishing to bore you with too many details, some of the examples I have to offer will make you think about your selections in Nursery races, which is surely the whole point in buying this book.

Windsor is a good venue to choose to make a study of two year-old races in general, as so many punters are influenced by the draw which usually favours high numbers in sprint races.

Horses on the wrong side dominated a finish of a Nursery race at Windsor in September last year, which devastated the live toteplacepot units after the event had been run.

Less than three per cent of all units won through (97.1% eliminated), and all because the runners on the stands side missed out on the places. Top juvenile trainers such as Jamie Osborne and Rod Millman saddled horses in the frame, whilst four favourites claimed toteplacepot positions in the other five races on the card, yet the toteplacepot dividend exceeded two thousand pounds!

Three favourites priced at 5/4 made the frame, with other horses at 13/8, 11/2 and 6/1, yet that marvellous dividend was declared.

Another meeting at Windsor in October had punters running for cover, as just 8.1% of toteplacepot clients made it through the opening (Nursery) event of the meeting.

Yes, Mark Johnston and David Loder saddled placed horses in that opening race but the beaten 6/4 favourite knocked the stuffing out of most investors. 91.9% of punters lost out, and they must have been cursing their luck as the next three favourites (including a 10/11 market leader) won their way through en route to a £1,445.80 dividend!

Before you suggest there must have been another race to wipe punters out, I can report a second favourite and a third market leader were placed in the other two races on the card.

Last year's Cambridgeshire result helped to create a toteplacepot dividend of over £4,000, at the respective meeting, but the damage had been done on the very first (Nursery) race.

Despite Richard Hannon and Neville Callaghan saddling placed horses in the race (as well as the third favourite winning the race), over 80% of the toteplacepot units went up in smoke.

A Yarmouth dividend of over £7,000 pounds was declared last October, and whilst only two favourites managed to make the frame during the course of the meeting, it's worth noting that over 90% of placepot units were lost after the first (Nursery) event.

The prices of the horses that filled the frame were 10/1, 15/2 and 16/1.

I suggest that you give Nursery races your full attention, whether you are making a single bet or investing in a toteplacepot wager.

MAKE SURE YOU DECIDE WHEN YOU ARE GOING TO HAVE A BET!

Nursery races form just part of the racing calendar, of course, and this last chapter applies to all betting scenarios, not just in the horse racing sector.

The mistake so many punters make is that they allow bookmakers to dictate the terms of betting, yet, with a little application, the general public can become as informed as the market makers.

Bookmakers are Turf Accountants by definition, and like any other accountant they simply have to balance their books.

Turf Accountants use percentages to dictate their transactions and there is no reason why you cannot become as mathematical in your approach to the betting war between bookmaker and punter.

The full percentage table is as follows:

ODDS ON%	PRICE	ODDS AGAINST%
50.0	EVS	50.0
52.4	11/10	47.6
54.5	6/5	45.5
55.6	5/4	44.4
57.9	1/8	42.1
60.0	6/4	40.0
61.9	13/8	38.1

NURSERY CLASS

ODDS ON%	PRICE	ODDS AGAINST%
63.6	7/4	36.4
65.2	15/8	34.8
66.7	2/1	33.3
69.2	9/4	30.8
71.4	2/5	28.6
73.3	11/4	26.7
75.0	3/1	25.0
76.9	10/3	23.1
77.8	7/2	22.2
80.0	4/1	20.0
81.8	9/2	18.2
83.3	5/1	16.7
84.6	11/2	15.4
85.7	6/1	14.3
86.7	13/2	13.3
87.5	7/1	12.5
88.3	15/2	11.7
88.9	8/1	11.1
89.5	17/2	10.5
90.0	9/1	10.0
90.9	10/1	9.1
91.7	11/1	8.3
92.3	2/1	7.7
93.3	14/1	6.7
94.1	16/1	5.9
94.7	18/1	5.3
95.2	20/1	4.8
95.8	22/1	4.2
96.2	25/1	3.8
96.6	28/1	3.4
97.0	33/1	3.0
97.6	40/1	2.4
98.0	50/1	2.0
98.5	66/1	1.5
98.8	80/1	1.2
99.0	100/1	1.0

You will quickly deduce that, by adding the odds on figure to the odds against percentage, the result is 100%, which is as it should be.

Next time you see a horse backed from 25/1 to 12/1 (a difference of 3.9%) in a Nursery event do not be alarmed. Now you are in full possession of the facts, you will quickly deduce that the comparison is roughly the same as a favourite being backed into 9/4 from 15/8 (a difference of 4.0%), which is exactly why you need to digest these figures.

If you didn't know before, you will now recognise that a potential runner at 8/1 for any race represents 11.1% of the market from the bookmaker's perspective.

Try to learn these figures parrot fashion if you can, or preferably, take a copy of these percentages with you when you wage war with the enemy, whether in a betting shop, on the internet, or on the racecourse!

Alternatively, you should be able to remember the figures if you round up/down the percentages to whole numbers, which will give you approximate details which are good enough to arm you with an important weapon against the bookmaker.

73.3% for example (4/11) would be rounded down to 73, whereas 26.7% (11/4 against) could be rounded up to 27.

You will be able to decide whether to back your judgement immediately when prices become available, having decided the odds that you are willing to accept BEFORE knowing the price which has been quoted.

Using this method, *you* are the one who is dictating the potential betting scenario, not the bookmaker.

Be lucky.

STOP PRESS!

I have avoided the temptation to tamper with the text regarding some of the horses that appear in this publication.

It would seem that the 2004 Nursery *crop* were a decent bunch, because as an example, I cannot believe that too many winners of two-year-old handicap races have gone on to finish second in the 2,000 Guineas (at 100/1) the following year, yet Rebel Rebel achieved that distinction following his 5/1 Easter Stakes victory at Kempton on his three-year-old debut.

Wise Dennis won just the one race in 2004, before landing a Listed race at York's *Dante* meeting at the rewarding odds of 9/1, whilst Coleorton Dancer scored at the first time of asking as a three-year-old at 14/1 at Ripon!

Crosspeace won a decent Newmarket handicap at odds of 9/2, whilst Im Spartacus was *touched off* by the minimum margin at 33/1 when thwarted by Gypsy King in the Group 3 Dee Stakes at Chester and won next time out at York at 9/4.

Obe Gold was possibly the first representative of the 2005 turf season when scoring at 4/1 on Kempton's card in March, whilst Come On Jonny won at 12/1 just three days later at Doncaster! Then Mimi Mouse at 16/1 on 14 May and as we go to print Toldo at 9/2 on 15 May.

Let's hope the winners continue to flood in.